IMAGES OF WAR
SS-TOTENKOPF FRANCE 1940

RARE PHOTOGRAPHS FROM WARTIME ARCHIVES

JACK HOLROYD

Pen & Sword
MILITARY

First published in Great Britain in 2012 by
PEN & SWORD MILITARY
an imprint of
Pen & Sword Books Ltd,
47 Church Street, Barnsley,
South Yorkshire.
S70 2AS

Copyright © Jack Holroyd, 2012

ISBN 978 1 84884 833 7

The right of Jack Holroyd to be identified as Author of this Work
has been asserted by him in accordance with the
Copyright, Designs and Patents Act 1988.

A CIP catalogue record for this book is available
from the British Library

*All rights reserved. No part of this book may be reproduced or transmitted
in any form or by any means, electronic or mechanical including photocopying,
recording or by any information storage and retrieval system,
without permission from the Publisher in writing.*

Printed and bound in Great Britain by CPI Group UK Ltd, Croydon, CR0 4YY

*Pen & Sword Books Ltd incorporates the imprints of
Pen & Sword Aviation, Pen & Sword Maritime,
Pen & Sword Military, Pen & Sword Select, Pen & Sword Military Classics,
Leo Cooper, Wharncliffe Local History*

For a complete list of Pen & Sword titles please contact:
PEN & SWORD BOOKS LIMITED
47 Church Street, Barnsley, South Yorkshire, S70 2AS, England.
E-mail: enquiries@pen-and-sword.co.uk
Website: www.pen-and-sword.co.uk

Contents

Introduction **4**

Chapter One
    Dachau – Model Concentration Camp **7**

Chapter Two
    Theodore Eicke 'Papa' of Cruelty **13**

Chapter Three
    Totenkopf – On the Heels of the Attackers **25**

Chapter Four
    Blooded in Action – Forged by Fire **35**

Chapter Five
    Other Weapons – Engineers and Support Troops **65**

Chapter Six
    Le Paradis – Atrocity against the Norfolks **77**

Chapter Seven
    Approaches to the Channel Coast **101**

Chapter Eight
    The Sea – A Goal Achieved **115**

    Appendices
        Order of Battle/Attrocities   **126**
        Progress of SS-Totenkopf through France   **127**

Introduction

AWARENESS of the dubious reputation of the *Waffen* SS came for me at the age of fifteen when an Estonian national came to work for a time at the small printing shop where I was serving my apprenticeship. It was 1953 and the most terrible conflict in world history had ended eight years earlier and Alvar Verlieht had a story to tell.

The Baltic State of Estonia had been invaded first by the Soviet Union in 1940 and was declared to be a 'Soviet socialist republic'. Sovietization of the country on the basis of instructions from Moscow took place. Over 20,000 people, deemed to be a threat to the regime, were deported. Inevitably that oppression created determined pockets of resistence. When in the following year Germany launched Operation Barbarossa and took on the Red Army, the *Wehrmacht* drove through Estonian territory on its *Blitzkrieg* thrust towards Leningrad. Red Army attrocities against the people multiplied as Estonian men who had avoided the Soviet deportations fought alongside the Germans as guerrillas known as *Metsavennad* (Forest Brothers).

My Germanic-looking workmate, Alvar Verlieht, had once been a Forest Brother; now he was on his way to Canada to begin a new life. As a youngster brought up amidst the sights and sounds of formations of bombers overhead, air raid warning sirens, exploding bombs (on Sheffield), convoys of lorry laden soldiers driving through the village and the excited voice of the Pathé News commentator at the local cinema reporting on the progress of the war, I was fascinated by the real live ex-warrior who had fought on the side of Hitler.

The Estonian SS-Legion was formed on 1 October 1942 in the Debica military training camp near Krakow. Alvar told of how one day he and his fellow unit of Forest Brothers found SS uniforms had been laid out on every one of the beds in their billet. To a man they refused to don that uniform. They would carry on fighting the Reds as Estonian nationals and not as lackeys of Himmler. In the naivete of youth I recall asking why he and his fellow warriors had refused to wear that uniform seeing as how it was so distinctive and smart. He just smiled and shook his head – and later I would know why. A reputation for sheer ruthlessness was becoming firmly associated with the *Schutzstaffel*. Some Estonians, who had at first welcomed the Germans as liberators, fled to Finland as it became all too obvious there was little to choose between Stalin's Soviets and Hitler's Nazis when it came to brutal oppression and frightfulness.

Collar badge of the Estonian SS-Legion.

The SS organization came into being in 1925 as an Assembly-Hall-Protection unit, it was intended as a security force for Nazi party meetings and as a personal protection squad for Adolf Hitler. Between 1929 and 1945 under the leadership of Heinrich Himmler it grew from a small paramilitary formation into one of the largest and most powerful organizations in the Third Reich. At the Nuremberg Trials in 1945 it was branded an illegal organization. Despite this, ex-members of the SS have continued to hold reunions and a strong bond of comradeship existed among them – the *Waffen* SS. This work, based around photographs and captions from 1940, will hopefully serve to explain how the terrible reputation of this military organization that was about to strike fear throughout Europe, saw its birth during the invasion of the Low Countries in 1940.

SS *Totenkopf*

This SS Division was formed in October 1939, initially, from concentration camp guards of the 1st (Oberbayern), 2nd (Brandenburg) and 3rd (Thüringen) regiments of the SS-*Totenkopfverbände*, and soldiers from the SS-*Heimwehr* Danzig. Some officers from the SS-*Verfügungstruppe* had seen action in Poland. The division's originator and commander was SS-*Obergruppenführer* Theodor Eicke.

The *Totenkopf* had missed the Polish campaign and was initially held in reserve during the assault on France and the Low Countries in May 1940. They were committed to a front-line assault on the 16 May. Immediately, the politically motivated *Totenkopf* soldiers began to suffer heavy losses as they fought with a fervour and dedication in excess to that of their *Wehrmacht* comrades. The Division's first war crime was carried out within days of being committed to front line action. At the French village of Le Paradis the *4th Kompanie, I Abteilung*, commanded by SS-*Obersturmführer* Fritz Knöchlein, machine-gunned ninety-nine British officers and men of the Norfolk Regiment after they had surrendered to them. Two victims survived the massacre and managed to crawl away and surrender to a *Wehrmacht* unit. After the war, Knöchlein was tried by a British Court and convicted for that war crimes. In 1948 he was sentenced to death and hanged.

Totenkopf saw action a number of times during the French campaign. To the north-east of Cambrai the Division took 16,000 French prisoners. Whilst subsequently trying to drive through to the coast they encountered a major Anglo-French force which they had a great deal of difficulty stopping and came perilously close to panic. *Totenkopf*, fighting alongside General Rommel's 7.*Panzerdivision*, had to resort to firing 88 mm anti-aircraft guns in an anti-tank role, and were saved by the intervention of Stuka dive-bombers. The Division went on to suffer heavily during the crossing of the La Bassée Canal. Further stiff resistance was encountered at both Béthune and particularly at Le Paradis, hence the massacre of the Norfolks.

Early days for the new military formation: A Czechoslovakian BRNO LMG operated by men of SS *Totenkopf* during training prior to the invasion of the Low Countries in May 1940.   TL/WW2 010

The French surrender found the Division located near the Spanish border, where it was to stay, resting and refitting, until April 1941. *Totenkopf* had suffered heavy losses during the campaign, including over 300 officers. Replacement personnel were supplied, this time via regular *Waffen*-SS recruitment as opposed to coming from concentration camp guards. Flak and artillery battalions were added to its strength. Vehicles were commandeered from the French, many of the division's soft-skinned transports during Barbarossa were of French origin. During the French campaign immediately equipment such as armoured cars and tanks were captured they had white crosses and swastikas daubed on and were put into action against their former owners. Interestingly, many weapons of the *Totenkopf* in 1940 were of Czech manufacture. Later Hitler saw to it that Himmler's *Waffen* SS were supplied with the best and latest weapons. This is the account of their first month of war.

Taylor collection
The German book *DAMAL* published in 1940-41 by SS Headquarters Office, Stuttgart, was a collaboration by SS War Correspondents Ege Hermann, Charles F. Bauer and Herbert Bonda. Their captions are euphoric and even excitable – understandably so – never had there been such a resounding victory by one major nation over the armies of two other modern powers, and in such a short time, as *Blitkrieg* swept all before it. Their writing is translated into English and represented here in italics so as to keep the flavour of the time. Additional illustrations have been included from the Taylor Library to help the pictorial history along and they, along with images from *DAMAL*, will serve as a catalogue for illustrations available in that archive. An identifying number is included in the captions.

Where appropriate, ranks and military formations are represented in their Germanic form so as to avoid pidgin-German terms (for example Panzer**s** rather than the correct plural form Panzer). These are set in italics.

Chapter One

Dachau – Model Concentration Camp

IN THE 1930s AND 40s communities throughout Germany had members taken away to internment camps. Regularly newspapers ran stories of 'the removal of the enemies of the Reich to concentration camps'. A rhyme became popular among the people of Hitler's Third Reich *'Lieber Gott, mach mich dumm, damit ich nicht nach Dachau kumm'* (Dear God, make me dumb, that I may not to Dachau come). Psychological terror was a weapon unleashed against its citizens. Dachau was the first camp set up in 1933 when Hitler came to power and was to become a model for the rest that would follow. German Communists and other political groups were the first targets followed by the hated *Bibelforscher* who refused to join the armed forces and to 'heil Hitler'; Jews, homosexuals and any individual or group that did not conform to the ideals of the new Germany were selected for containment and punishment.

The organization and layout of Dachau was developed by *Kommandant* Theodor Eicke and went on to be applied to all later camps that were set up throughout Germany and occupied territories. Eicke became the chief inspector for all concentration camps, responsible for molding the rest according to the model of his creation. *'Arbeit macht frei'* (through work one will be free), was the slogan over the entrance gate to his camps, and in the majority of individual instances was a mockery.

> **'On Wednesday the first concentration camp is to be opened in Dachau with an accommodation for 5,000 people. All Communists and, where necessary, Reichsbanner and Social Democratic functionaries who endanger state security are to be concentrated here, as in the long run it is not possible to keep individual functionaries in the state prisons without overburdening these prisons, and on the other hand these people cannot be released because attempts have shown that they persist in their efforts to agitate and organise as soon as they are released.'**
>
> Press statement issued to the newspapers at the opening of Dachau, 22 March 1933.

Subsequently, the camp was used for prisoners of all sorts from every nation occupied by the forces of the Third Reich. After the war up until 1948 the camp continued to be used as a prison for SS officers awaiting trial for war crimes. After 1948 the German population expelled from Czechoslovakia were housed there and it was also a base employed by the United

New arrivals at Dachau concentration camp, March 1933. TL/WW2 001

German Communists on arrival at Dachau concentration camp awaiting to be processed into the system. TL/WW2 002

Inspection by the Nazi party and Himmler at Dachau on 8 May 1936. *Kommandant* Theodore Eiche can be seen over Himmler's left shoulder. TL/WW2 003

Main prisoners' compound with a guard tower in the distance. TL/WW2 003

States. It was closed in 1960 and thereafter, at the insistence of ex-prisoners, various memorials began to be constructed.

History will never know exactly how many people were interned there or died as a result of executions, beatings, starvation, disease and suicides. Certainly during the Third Reich's years over 200,000 prisoners were interned at Dachau from more than thirty countries of whom two-thirds were political prisoners and nearly one-third were Jews. Over 25,500 prisoners are believed to have died in the camp and almost another 10,000 in its subcamps. As the war came to an end death marches to and from the camp accounted for the deaths of a further unknown number of prisoners. Former inmates weakened beyond recovery continued to die, even after the liberation in the summer of 1945.

The German military used the Soviet Union's refusal to sign the Geneva Convention as a reason for not providing the necessities of life to Russian POWs. This also led to further attrocities and in 1941 and 1942 an unknown number of Soviet prisoners of war were executed by shooting at Dachau's firing ranges.

Dachau, along with Auschwitz, came to symbolize the Nazi concentration camps to many people. *Konzentrationslager* (KZ) Dachau holds a vivid place in public memory because it was the second camp to be liberated by British or American forces. Consequently, it was one of the first places where these previously unknown Nazi practices were exposed to the British and American public in the cinemas through the newsreels.

DAILY CAMP ROUTINE

04.00	Reveille. Make beds and clean barracks.
05.15	Parade for roll call
06.15	Detailed to work
12.00	Mid-day meal
13.00	Back to work
18.30	End of working day
19.00	Evening roll call
20.00	Meal
21.00	Lights out

Winter time and the day began one hour later. Work stopped at nightfall. Roll call could take upwards of an hour and punishments were carried out on the parade ground in front of the prisoners.

Prisoners were in a constant state of apprehension. There was little free time, prisoners were not allowed visitors and letters were heavily censored.
TL/WW2 005

One prisoner raises a smile for the guard with the camera while the others prefer to remain unrecognized. In the early days, work carried out by the prisoners was deliberately contrived by the SS guards to break the spirit; tedious and pointless tasks such as moving piles of rocks backwards and forwards went on all day.
TL/WW2 006

'Work Brings Freedom' was the slogan worked in wrought iron of the camp gate.
TL/WW2 009

Head of the German Labour Front, Robert Ley, inspects the concentration camp guards at Dachau. From among these men the *Kommandant*, Theodore Eicke, would raise a nucleous for a new motorized infantry division – SS *Totenkopf*. TL/WW2 008

Papa Eicke
That's the name, given him by his men. That is his name of honor.
Obergruppenführer Eicke, commander of the SS Totenkopf Division
He became a father to his men.
He was their paternal friend in grave times and in happy days.
Hard and firm in combat, open-minded and with sincere kindness when dealing with the personal matters of his men,
Our Papa Eicke
From the above it would seem that his men thought the world of him.
TL/WW2 SSTrps 93

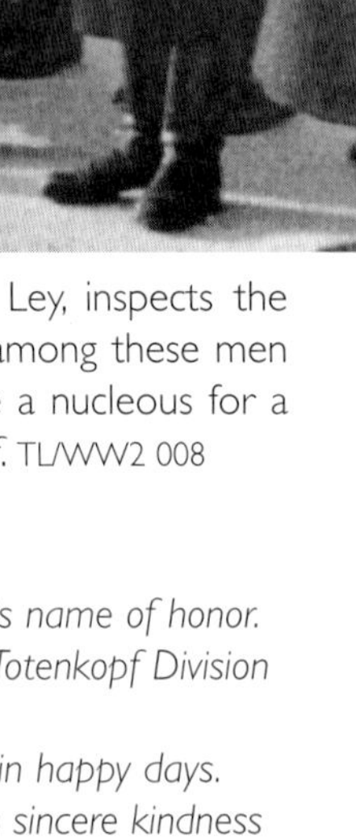

Death's head insignia adopted for Himmler's new division the SS-*Totenkopf*.

Chapter Two

Theodor Eicke 'Papa' of Cruelty

NO PITY WAS to be shown for enemies of the state and prisoners were treated with the utmost cruelty, and in Theodor Eicke the Nazi leaders had found the right man for the job when it came to promoting terror. It was Eicke who laid down detailed instructions and methods on corporal punishment, summary beatings, solitary confinement and shooting of offenders who were considered to be agitators, mutineers or reactionary elements who refused to obey instructions (usually totally unreasonable) regarding work details.

On 14 November 1939 he was appointed Commander of the first SS-*Totenkopf Division* which he formed in Dachau with his camp guards as the cadre for the new formation. Also he took over the organization and employment of the *Totenkopfverebände* which saw active service in Poland and with these he was able to stiffen his new command of fighting troops.

His position as head of the concentration camps made him the most powerful SS leader second to Himmler in the country.

During the Polish campaign he served as the Head of the Police and SS assigned to the areas of *Armeeoberkommando 8* and *10* (note the 10 on his cuff title). Following the victory over the Polish forces his office of oversight became the HSSPF Ost (East) in the General Government area of Poland.

TL/Eicke015

Theodor Eicke

Son of a railway stationmaster born in Hamport, Alsace, October, 17 1892. Youngest of eleven children.

1. Volunteered for army in 1909.
2. Served in an infantry regiment in 1914.
3. Transferred to the artillery in 1916.
4. He served as a paymaster throughout his service.
5. Left army in March 1919 with rank of *Unterzahlmeister* (under pay master).
6. Awarded Iron Cross 2nd class; Brunswick War Service Cross 2nd class; Bavarian Order of Merit 2nd class; Bavarian Military Service Badge 3rd Class.
7. Enlisted in police in 1919 but was dismissed for political agitation against the Weimar Republic in July 1920.
8. Obtained a post with police administration in Ludwigshafen am Rhein but was dismissed in January 1923 due to his radical views.
9. Worked at I.G. Farben from January 1923 to March 1932.
10. In 1928 he joined the NSDAP and the SA.
11. On 20 July 1930 he transferred to the SS where he found an outlet for his extreme right wing views.
12. He worked his way through the SS ranks until in November 1931 he was promoted to SS-*Sturmbahnführer*.
13. He was arrested in March 1932 when he attempted to obtain explosives. He was sentenced to two years but did not serve his sentence.
14. He was assigned by Himmler to oversee a refugee camp in Italy for five months.
15. In trouble when, during a march celebrating the anniversary of the Fascist march on Rome, he led an SS detachment in the parade. The Austrians demanded that he be severely punished.
16. Eicke escaped to Thuringia to avoid punishment.
17. On his word to behave himself he was allowed to return to his home in Ludwigshafen.
18. There was further trouble in his home town when he joined a mutiny against the local branch of the NSDAP.
19. Himmler was furious and dismissed him from the SS for failure to improve his conduct.
20. Himmler had Eicke committed to a mental institution to try and keep a lid on him.
21. Despite this, upon his release on 26 June 1933, he was taken back into the SS with his previous rank.
22. In 1934 he was assigned a post on Himmler's staff and took over command of Dachau concentration camp.
23. At the time of the purge of the SA leadership – 'Night of the Long Knives' – its was Eicke who shot Ernst Röhm in his prison cell 1 July 1934.

In July 1941, in Russia, he was wounded when his staff car ran over a mine. He returned to take command of his Division once more two months later, having recovered from a badly injured foot and nerve damage. He was made a *General der Waffen SS* and at Christmas time, 1941, was awarded the Knight's Cross for his leadership at the Lowat and Pola Rivers along with the bitter fighting at Luschino. Eiche led the *Totenkopf* in the fighting in the Demjansk pocket which resulted in him being awarded the Oakleaves and his immediate promotion to SS-*Obergruppenfürer und General der Waffen-SS*. On 26 June 1942 Hitler presented him with his Oakleaves decoration at the Führer headquarters at Rastenberg.

Eicke continued as the commander of the division when it was enlarged and re-equipped to become a *Panzergrenadierdivision* in 1942.

Eicke was killed when his observation plane was shot down by a Soviet fighter in February 1943.

Eicke surrounded by his officers. From among these he would form his fighting division SS *Totenkopf*, many of the officers subsequently going on to serve in positions of responsiblity within the SS organization. TL/Eicke017

TL/Bochmann021

TL/Brasack022

Georg Bochmann, former member of the *Hitlerjugend*, was commissioned as an SS-*Untersturmführer* (Second Lieutenant) in April 1936. He received training at Dachau concentration camp. Before the invasion of Poland Theodor Eicke recommended him for promotion to SS-*Hauptsturmführer* (Captain). When the *Totenkopf* Division was formed he commanded *14.Infanterie Regiment*. He was wounded five times and was highly decorated being awarded the Knight's Cross with Oakleaves and Swords. He was removed from his command for refusing to lead a suicidal attack. However, Hitler gave him command of the *17.SS-Panzergrenadierdivision 'Götz von Berlichingen'*. He surrendered his command to the US Army, on 9 May 1945. He died at Offenbach am Main, in June 1973 at the age of sixty.

Kurt Brasack was a *leutnant* in the First World War and was a holder of the Iron Cross. He enlisted in the SS in 1931 as an SS-*Mann*. After training with the army he became an SS-*Obersturmbannführer* (Lieutenant Colonel) December 1939 and assigned to the *Totenkopf* as commander of *I./SS Totenkopf Artillerie Regiment*. He continued to commanded that artillery regiment until May 1941. He went on to serve in other SS divisions: WIKING, REICH, DAS REICH, and NEDERLAND. His final command and rank was that of SS-*Brigadeführer* (Brigadier) with *IV.SS Panzer Korps*. He was awarded clasps to his First World War Iron Crosses and the German Cross in Gold. He was captured by the US Army and finally released in 1949. He died in Hamburg in 1978 at the age of eighty-six.

TL/Deisenhofer023

TL/Lammerding024

Eduard Deisenhofer was promoted to SS-*Scharführer* (Colour Sergeant) in 1932. He quickly passed through the ranks and in 1934 was commissioned as an SS-*Obersturmführer* (Lieutenant). After training at Dachau he took command of a company-size formation. A year before war broke out he was promoted to SS-*Sturmbannführer* (Major) and became an officer in the newly forming *Totenkopf Division*. He was wounded in May 1940 during the invasion of the Low Countries. He went on to serve with the Division on the Eastern Front where he was severely wounded again in November 1941 by a grenade. He recruited for the *Waffen* SS in Rumania in September 1944. Promoted to SS-*Oberführer* (Colonel) in January 1945 he was killed in action later that month at the age of thirty-six.

Heinz Lammerding was formerly a member of the SA and went on to teach combat engineering. With the creation of the *Totenkopf* in October 1939 he became commander of its *Pioneer Bataillon* with the rank of SS-*Sturmbannführer* (Major). During the attack on Belgium and France he was awarded both classes of the Iron Cross. He served on the Eastern Front having been promoted to SS-*Standartenführer* (Colonel) and was involved in the anti-partisan fighting before going on to command a *Kampfgruppe*. He was transfered to the West and given command of the SS-*Das Reich Division* with the rank of SS-*Brigadeführer* (Brigadier). During the Normandy fighting he was wounded. He was tried by the French for the massacre at Oradour-sur-Glane but he died of cancer in January 1971 aged sixty-six.

TL/Lombard025 TL/Petersen026

Gustav Lombard, was in the United States during the First World War and was interned, returning to Germany in 1931. He joined the Nazi Party in 1933 and later the SS where he received a commission as SS-*Untersturmführer* (Second Lieutenant) in 1934. Following periods of training with the Army he received a further promotion and transferred to the *1.SS-Totenkopf Reiterstandarte* in February 1940. He was awarded the Knight's Cross in 1943 and in the following year, 1944, he was engaged in anti-partisan operations with the rank of SS-*Brigadeführer* (Brigadier). His final assignment was commander of the *31.SS-Freiwilligen Grenadierdivision*. With the war's end he was taken prisoner by the Russians and was not released until 1955. He died in September 1992 aged ninety-seven.

Heinrich Petersen served in the German Army between wars where he reached the rank of *Oberfeldwebel* (Sergeant-major). In 1933 he joined the SS and served as an instructor at *SS-Führerschule Bad Tölz* receiving a commission as an *Untersturmführer* and later as SS-*Obersturmführer* (Lieutenant). At that time he was also an officer in the *Wehrmacht* with the rank of *Oberlieutnant*. With the formation of the *Totenkopf* Division he was given command of *II/SS-Totenkopf Infanterieregiment 3*. He was awarded the Iron Cross 2nd Class and then 1st Class in May and June 1940. He was transferred to *SS-Freiwilligen-Gebirgs 'Prinz Eugen'* and fought the partisans in Yugoslavia, transferring to the *18.SS-Panzergrenadier Division 'Horst Wessel'*. He committed suicide in Czechoslovakia, on 9 May 1945, nine days after Hitler. He was forty-one years old.

TL/Priess027

TL/Richter028

Hermann Priess joined the SS in 1933 and received a commission in 1935. He was promoted to SS-*Obersturmführer* (Lieutenant) in 1935 as a machine gun platoon leader. He attended an artillery training school with the Army and was promoted to SS-*Sturmbannführer* (Major) in June 1939. He saw service in Poland in 1939 as part of Panzer Division *KEMPF* winning both classes of the Iron Cross. With the formation of *Totenkopf* Priess and his unit were brought in to form the artillery cadre. Following the Battle of France he was promoted to SS-*Obersturmbannführer*. He led the *Totenkopf* artillery regiment in Russia winning the Knight's Cross and later the Oakleaves and Swords. He was captured by US forces and tried for the Malmedy massacre and released in 1954. He died in 1985 aged eighty-four.

Joachim Richter served in the First World War and was awarded the Iron Cross (both classes). He was a leading member of the veteran organization *Stahlhelm* but left in order to join the SS in 1933. He served in the *Allgemeine* with the rank of SS-*Standartenführer* transferring to the *Waffen-*SS in 1939. He was assigned as an artillery battery commander in the *Totenkopf* at its formation. He remained with the *Totenkopf* until 1941 when he transferred to the *WIKING* Division as commander of *II./Artillerieregiment*. He spent the rest of the war on the Eastern Front reaching the rank of SS-*Standartenführer* (Colonel) and winning the Knight's Cross in 1944. He commanded the *32.SS-Freiwillige Grenadierdivision '30 Januar'* before being assigned to the staff of the SS-*Personalhauptamt* in 1945. He died in 1970 at the age of seventy-four.

TL/Simon029

TL/Strange030

Max Simon saw action the First World War in Macedonia and the Western Front and went on to serve in the post war Freikorps. He joined the SS in 1933 receiving a commission. When the *Totenkopf* was formed he became commander of *SS-Totenkopf Infanterieregiment 1* and was promoted to SS-*Standartenführer* (Colonel) in September 1938. For his service on the Western Front in 1940 he was awarded the Knight's Cross. He assumed command of the Division when Eicke was killed in 1943. A disciplined follower of Eicke, Max Simon was sentenced to death by the British for the killing of civilians in Italy. This was commuted to life and he was released in 1954. The Russians also wanted him for killings in Kharkov. The postwar German authorites also brought charges. While awaiting trial he died in 1961 aged sixty-two.

Martin Stange joined the SS in 1933 and two years later was commissioned as an SS-*Untersturmführer* and in 1936 promoted to SS-*Obersturmführer* (Lieutenant). Following training with the Army he transferred to the SS-*Verfügungstruppe* and fought in Poland in command of an *Artillerie Regiment Batterie* winning the Iron Cross. When the *Totenkopf* was formed in 1939 he was transferred along with his unit to form a cadre and became commander of *7.Batterie*. After a period on the Eastern Front he became a lecturer at SS-*Junkerschule* Bad Tölz in 1943 with the rank of SS-*Obersturmbannführer* (Lieutenant Colonel). He joined *16.SS-Panzergrenadierdivision 'Reichsführer SS'* finishing the war commanding the final cadet class at Bad Tölz employed in action against the Americans. Martin Strange was born in 1910.

A *Totenkopf* artillery unit receives instruction on firing a 10.5 cm howtizer from German Army officers during a prewar training exercise.
TL/WW2 015

Men of the *Totenkopf* bringing a Pak 36 anti-tank gun into postion during pre-war manouevres. This is an early model, an obsolete weapon used for training puposes.
TL/WW2 014

A patrol passes through a line of their comrades during a training exercises. The then innovative camouflage smocks and helmet covers gave the SS a professional and business-like appearance.
TL?WW2 012

This team is equipped with a BRNO LMG operated by men of SS *Totenkopf* who are seen here on a prewar training exercise.
TL?WW2 011

Learning how to use the 8-cm *schwere Granatwerfer* 34 or 8 cm sGrW 34 (heavy grenade-launcher model 1934). TL?WW2 013

SS-Obergruppenführer Eicke commander of SS-Totenkopf Division in his staff car on the way to the front. Blitzkrieg on the Low Countries would sweep through the Allies. SS Trps01

Chapter Three

Totenkopf – on the Heels of the Attackers

HAVING MISSED THE POLISH CAMPAIGN, and therefore the necessary combat experience, *Totenkopf* was held in reserve during the initial assault into France and the Low Countries on 10 May 1940. Eicke had pressed for his division to be employed in the crucial opening attack of *Fall Gelbe* (Case Yellow), however, this was deemed unwise by the Chief of the Army General Staff, Franz Halder, declaring that they would find 'a battle of weapons a difficult undertaking'. They were committed to action in Belgium six days into the invasion, alongside *5.Panzerdivision* and *7.Panzerdivision*. They encountered no opposition driving through Holland and Belgium on the heels of the attacking formations of the German Army. On 19 May Eicke received orders from *XV Panzer Korps* to move into France and head for Le Cateau. *7.Panzerdivision* had been pinned down by a French counter-attack.

The *Totenkopf* had been called upon to support a crack division of the *Wehrmacht* commanded by General Erwin Rommel. Eicke ordered an attack across the River Sambre where his men came up against Moroccan troops and vicious hand-to-hand fighting occurred. By 20 May the way was clear for the armour to continue. The *Totenkopf* had taken 1,600 prisoners, weapons, vehicles and equipment in its first engagement.

> When I see the national flag in the wind
> I get so proud of what I believe in
> I feel so strong I can do whatever I like
> To do whatever I want and I know it's right
> There is nothing like it to see the flag in the wind
> There is nothing like it so go out there and win.
>
> TOTENKOPF BATTLE SONG

As follow-up troops in reserve they follow on the heels of the attacking divisions. Here they pause as they cross the Belgian-French border where they note that the fronts of the bunkers and field positions are constructed so as to face a threat from the east only. Germany was always deemed to be the enemy.

Original captions: *Fortifications abandoned by its defenders in hopeless flight. Farmers have evacuated to the west leaving their cattle to the invaders.*

Man and machine are camouflaged against air attack. However, Stukas of the *Luftwaffe* rule the skies over France and Belgium in 1940. The officers are in a 4×2 Kfz.12 (Adler 3Gd) 6-cylinder staff car; they confer with a motorcyclist despatch rider mounted on a BMW (2-cylinder, 18 bhp, 750-cc OHV shaft-driven engine with a maximum speed of 110 km per hour). SSTrps06

The caption for this picture translates: *We have taught our enemies how to run and our Stukas will make sure they receive constant reminders.* SS men of an anti-tank unit survey recent damage caused by their supporting dive bombers. The vehicle is a 6x4 Krupp L2H143 light truck. SSTrps07

Original caption: *Cautiously, an advance party puts out feelers before rolling into town.* Men of the *Totenkopf* move into a deserted French town. The vehicle is a 6-cylinder medium car, Kfz 11 ('Wanderer' W23S). SSTrps08

Judged to be safe from surprises, more men move quickly through the streets past the remnants of a hastely constructed and now abandoned baracade. SSTrps09

SS men grab a rest and a smoke on a French river bank. The original caption: *Every free minute is used to gather strength for further action. And a 'stick' between the lips of the weary and their spirits are refreshed once more.* SSTrps13

Left: the original caption reads: *The hot sun burns down from the bright blue sky of France as our men advance up steep roads and paths. Sweat trickles into streams over sunburned, dust-covered faces; helmets off, sleeves rolled up, there is just no stopping them – forward – ever onward.* SSTrps10

These former concentration camp guards have been singled out by the *Totenkopf* photographer who wrote his caption as follows: *Among our men quite a few show grey hair at their temples. Many of our comrades were thought by the British to be 'only' reservists, however, these volunteers from the Allgemeine-SS soon proved to the Tommies what they were made of.* These then were certainly men encouraged to act in a harsh and an uncompromising manner towards those who were deemed enemies of the Third Reich. Regularly they would have administered beatings and all manner of violence to the unfortunates in their charge. Little wonder that dreadful attrocities occurred wherever they served as fighting troops of the *Waffen-SS*. SSTrps11

'Papa' Eicke with one of his officers. The original caption: *The 'Old Man' in the front line discussing the situation with one of his commanders.* The caption draws attention to the officer with Eicke: *Note this leader of an SS unit is carrying a rifle and looks as if he has been in the thick of it judging from the torn epaulette on his right shoulder.* SSTrps23

Our comrades from the military police will guide us through the rubble of the shattered towns and villages.

Fighting has moved on and once more civilians are venturing onto the streets.

Chapter Four

Blooded in Action – Forged by Fire

IN THEIR VERY FIRST contact with the enemy Eicke's men found they were fighting against an 'inferior race' (according to the racial laws and beliefs then being enforced within Hitler's Germany) – French Moroccan soldiers. Several small villages were being defended by them and had to be cleared in a series of frontal attacks which, in many cases, resulted in fierce hand-to-hand fighting for the *Herrenvolk* ('master race'). Their eventual victory could only have confirmed feelings among Eicke's men of racial superiority over the inferior *Untermenschen* (sub-humans) from Africa. There follows a translation of the gung-ho rhetoric which accompanied the images of the *Totenkopf* engaged in action for the first time:

Man and the weapon must become fused into one. Whether rifle, pistol, machine gun or even an engineer's construction tools, no matter what the individual in this struggle has to handle – his weapon – must become an extension of his hands. Does that

include the artillery piece some might ask? Even the gun of the artillery becomes a comrade. Every man must be able to feel 'her', his weapon, automatically, instinctively, not having to think too much about its use. When he masters this he has little need to ask about the 'hows' the 'wheres' and 'whens' in battle.

Quiet was the man behind his machine gun as he blazed away at the enemy's pinpoints of fire. Our anti-tank gunners fired with practised precision when they spotted an enemy tank in their sights. A shot – was the enemy's armour pierced? As a blazing torch before them the tank erupted into flames. A grim smile touched the lips of the shooter – he has his marksmanship confirmed and he remains calm, that's certainly how it happens. He experiences a surge of confidence and is reassured when he knows for a certainty that he can rely on his weapon.

Rely on yourself if you must, but certainly on your comrades, and on the weapon in your hand which has already proved itself. How does that make you feel inside?

Original caption: *The column halts, thick smoke is rising from behind the grove of trees behind them. What does this mean? Binoculars sweep the terrain looking for some indication of the cause.* SSTrps15

These *Totenkopf* officers oblige the photographer and pose as if engaged in a crisis conference; an image intended for home consumption. The caption reads: *Quickly, the unit leaders have come together to discuss the situation. With the aid of the map a decision is made as to the continued direction of the advance in line with orders as laid down.* SSTrps16

On the evening of 19 May, 1940 the Division received the following order:
'Advance units of the *Totenkopf* Division must arrive at all speed by 05.00 hrs at the latest. It will proceed as far as Favril. After crossing the Sambre near

A Panzer towing a *Totenkopf* howitzer into a position where it cooudl give support to Rommel's 7.Panzerdivision. SSTrps30

Landrecies it is to attack in regimental strength in the direction of Le Chateau. It is to restore the situation where our forces are pinned down between Landrecies and Le Chateau and being attacked from the north. Seriousness of the situation for the 7.Panzerdivision requires that the attack begins punctually despite any state of exhaustion experienced by the relieving force. Anti-tank weapons must be brought up in large numbers and employed to the front. Upon arrival the regiment will be subordinated to the 7.Panzerdivision. The regimental commander must report to the divisional command post in La Bassee Narvilles, south of Neroilles.'

The commander of SS-*Totenkopf Infanterieregiment 1*, (which unit was now referred to by the Germans as 'Regiment Simon'), *SS-Standartenführer* Max Simon, issued his orders:

'Reinforced I/SS-Totenkopf Infanterieregiment 1 will proceed to the area of Catillon where it will engage the enemy. Reinforced II/SS-Totenkopf Infanterieregiment 1 is to take the village of Labre Guise, St Saplet and the village south of it. The reinforced III/SS-Totenkopf Infanterieregiment 1 is to occupy an area

in the line at Ribeauville-Castle Calondries with the purpose of guarding against a flank attack and to prevent enemy forces withdrawing from Catillon.'

When Max Simon arrived with his 'beefed-up' regiment to reinforce the panzer division and alleviate the pressure on it, General Rommel, commanding 7.Panzerdivision, informed him that his engineering battalion and some reconnaissance troops were struggling to throw the enemy back from along the la Sambre-Canal – Catillon line. Also, that the enemy was employed in strength and supported by artillery, heavy machine guns and anti-tank guns. The villages of Labre de Guise and St Saplet were also occupied by strong enemy forces who were holding up the advance.

At that point orders were received from XV.Armeekorps headquarters restating the critical position and what Max Simon's composite regiment was expected to do to relieve the *impasse* being created:

Major General Erwin Rommel, commander of 7.Panzerdivision.

SS-*Standartenführer* Max Simon, commander of SS-*Totenkopf Infanterieregiment 1*. TLWW2MaxSimon001

'Resolve the situation where our forces are pinned down and threatened by enemy attacks from the north. The seriousness of the situation for the 7.Panzerdivision makes it necessary to begin operations immediately, in spite of any exhaustion caused by the advance to the start line.'

After a sixteen hours march *SS-Regiment Simon* went into the attack against determined opposition which included action against British and French tanks.

French Renault B1bis at their start line ready for the order to attack. TLWW2hars001

Sheaves of corn provide cover for these artillery spotters. SSTrps017

A bolt of lightning and a thunder clap! Shells go howling over in salvos to shake the British Tommies out of their beds. SSTrps018

The *Totenkopf* cameraman covers the clearing of a French village and writes his jingoistic caption: *View from street level; 'Attention!' The village appears to be clear of the enemy, but it must be checked, for they must not be allowed time to rest. 'Next!' Pursuit of the enemy, and the wedge is driven deeper and deeper into the opponent's territory.* SSTrps78

Origin caption: *Prepared for action, safety catches are off and weapons are at the ready should any firing break out.* **SSTrps71**

A series of photographs depict the *Totenkopf* arriving in lorries and checking a village for signs of enemy occupation. The original caption: *Truck after truck rolls through the streets of what appears to be an abandoned village. However, our troops are ready for action with weapons at the ready. Suddenly there are a couple of shots from trapped enemy troops. Resistance? Bayonets flash brightly in the sun and quickly our men are out of their vehicles; all exit points from the village are covered by machine guns; all roads are secured. Thorough house to house searches begin and the gardens combed cleaned. The entire place is scoured and the enemy rear guards located and brought out as prisoners. 'Achtung!'. The village is free of the enemy, but there is no stopping, for the enemy must not be allowed to come to rest and form a defence line. 'Next!' Pursuit of the enemy, and the wedge is driven deep into the opponent.*

A couple of shots are fired. Resistance? Bayonets gleam dully in the sun. In no time the men are down from their vehicles. SSTrps72

A thorough search is made from house to house and the gardens are combed to ensure the entire village is clear. SSTrps74

Quickly, machine guns are set up at strategic points until all the roads in and out of the village have been covered. SSTrps73

Two French soldiers have been captured – remnants of the rearguard of the fleeing enemy. SSTrps75

Mount up! The village is free of the enemy and now we have to prevent further enemy troops from having time to rest and gather themselves.
The *Totenkopf* hurry to mount their 4 x 4 Opel Blitz trucks in the relentless non-stop thrust westward. SSTrps77

The caption for this photograph extols the camaraderie between the *Totenkopf* and the *Wehrmacht*: *There is a very warm sense of brotherhood between us and the men of 7.Panzerdivision which has a reputation for speedy advance. After all, we have to support each other closely.* SSTrps12
The *Totenkopf* had arrived in time to support Rommel's troops against a determined counter-attack. Rommel and his tank commanders hold a briefing in a corn field.

SS-*Standartenführer* Max Simon, commander of SS-*Totenkopf Infanterieregiment 1* confers with fellow officers prior to his unit's advance into the Arras sector. TLWW2Simon005

British Matilda II of the type which threatened the Panzer corridor south of Arras, 21 May 1940. The *Totenkopf* and Rommel's *7.Panzerdivision* were severely shaken when these heavily armoured tanks suddenly appeared on their flank. TLWW2Matilda001

Fast, all-terrain trucks bring our anti-tank guns into position. Speed often means victory. SSTrps57

'Pak to the front!' At a bend in the road and like the very devil himself, the vehicle dashes forward and within seconds the Pak is ready for action. The 37 mm Pak 35/36 is being towed by a Demag D7. SSTrps58

Men of *Totenkopf's* anti-tank unit swing a 37 mm Pak into position in an attempt to halt the Allied tanks. As quick as a weasel and inspired by unbridled aggression are these men of the Pak battalion. Every moment counts and within a matter of seconds they are ready to fire. SSTrps094

'Ready to fire!' Their gun disguised by a couple of old sacks and a weathered wooden frame these guys crouch behind their anti-tank gun. SSTrps095

Totenkopf anti-tank crew were staggered to see their shells bouncing off the British tanks. It was as if their 3.7 cm Pak 35/36s were merely acting as door knockers. A new name was born for their ineffective anti-tank gun – '*Türklopfer*' (doorknocker).

Even the cheaply produced two-man British Intantry tank, Matilda I, could take a direct hit from a 37 mm Pak 35/36 and survive.

'Signs of panic'

Commander of the German *XIX Korps*, General Heinz Guderian, made a comment in his memoirs concerning the British counter-attack at Arras, 21 May 1940: 'British armour launched an attack which came up against the *SS-Totenkopf Division*, which troops had little experience of combat and showed signs of panic. The British did not break through but they did make a considerable impression on the staff of *Panzergruppe Kleist* which suddenly became remarkably nervous.'

British reserves which had been assembled under the command of Major General Harold Franklyn to bolster the Allied defences in and around Arras were suddenly ordered to prepare for an offensive action. The force, which consisted of two divisions the 50th, 5th and 1st Army tank Brigade was named 'Frankforce' after its commanding general.

Perfectly calm, despite enemy fire, is our man crouched behind his E-meter rangefinder calculating the exact distance to the target for the artillery. SSTrps27

The counterattack at Arras was an Allied attempt to cut through the German spearhead and frustrate the German advance towards the Channel coast. Because of the many mechanical breakdowns, the tanks having had to drive 125 miles, there were just fifty-eight Mark Is, sixteen Mark IIs and seven Mark VIs available for the attack. The French had promised support and and some tanks were in position.

The attack hit the flank of 7.*Panzerdivision* and the *Totenkopf* taking them completely by surprise. At one sector Rommel was on hand to personally direct the defence:

> 'I brought every available gun into action at top speed against the tanks. Every gun, both anti-tank and anti-aircraft, was ordered to open rapid fire at once... With enemy tanks so perilously close only rapid fire from every gun could save the situation... Some gun commanders protested that the range was to great, but I overruled them... SS units close by had to fall back under the weight of the tank attack. Finally the anti-aircraft guns succeeded in bringing the enemy tanks to a halt.'

The crisis was over and officers and men of the *Totenkopf*, after having experienced feelings of panic, had acquired more battle experience.

An 88 mm flak gun firing in the anti-tank role during the Allied attack. Totenkopf officers and NCOs look on. SSTrps19

Frankforce Matilda tanks on fire after being stopped by anti-aircraft guns during their abortive attack against the German Panzer thrust to the coast. TLWW2Matilda11 003

A massive fortress of iron and steel that came crashing through the forest was located, knocked-out and now lies shrouded in smoke. A French Char B burning in a wood south of Arras. SSTrps60

Soldiers of *SS-Totenkopf* examining a captured British tank. *All knocked out enemy tanks will be examined closely as we need to keep learning: where is the decisive shot that caused it to stop? What effect did the impact of our shells have on the armour plate?*
This is a Matilda Mk II of the 7th Royal Tank Regiment, with its turret traversed 190 degrees and its main armament, 40 mm (two-pounder), pointed to the rear. The shell that stopped it (likely an 88) may have struck the engine compartment. Crew hatches are open which indicates that some of the crew may have escaped. SSTrps59

55

Totenkopf despatch riders in the village of Adinfer nine miles south of Arras. At the corner behind them is a PzKpfw 38(t) belonging to 7.*Panzerdivision*. These men await despatches from SS-*Standartenführer* Max Simon, commander of SS-*Totenkopf Infanterieregiment* 1. TLWW2desp001

Left: *Portrait of one of our despatch riders. Their lonely and dangerous job involves driving at speed through the countryside, often in enemy territory, back and forth with t despatches, communicating between headquarters and ou advancing units.* SSTrps63

Opposite: *Regimental command headquarters – this is w decisions are made and orders are then sent via radios, fie telephones and despatch riders to the fighting units keepir constant flow of information between the battalions and divisional headquarters. It is comparable to the human bro which oversees and commands the limbs of the body. Commander Max Simon can be seen in a discussion w his officers. Another officer can be seen (left) grabbing bite to eat. The motorcycle is a BMW R12.* SSTrps62

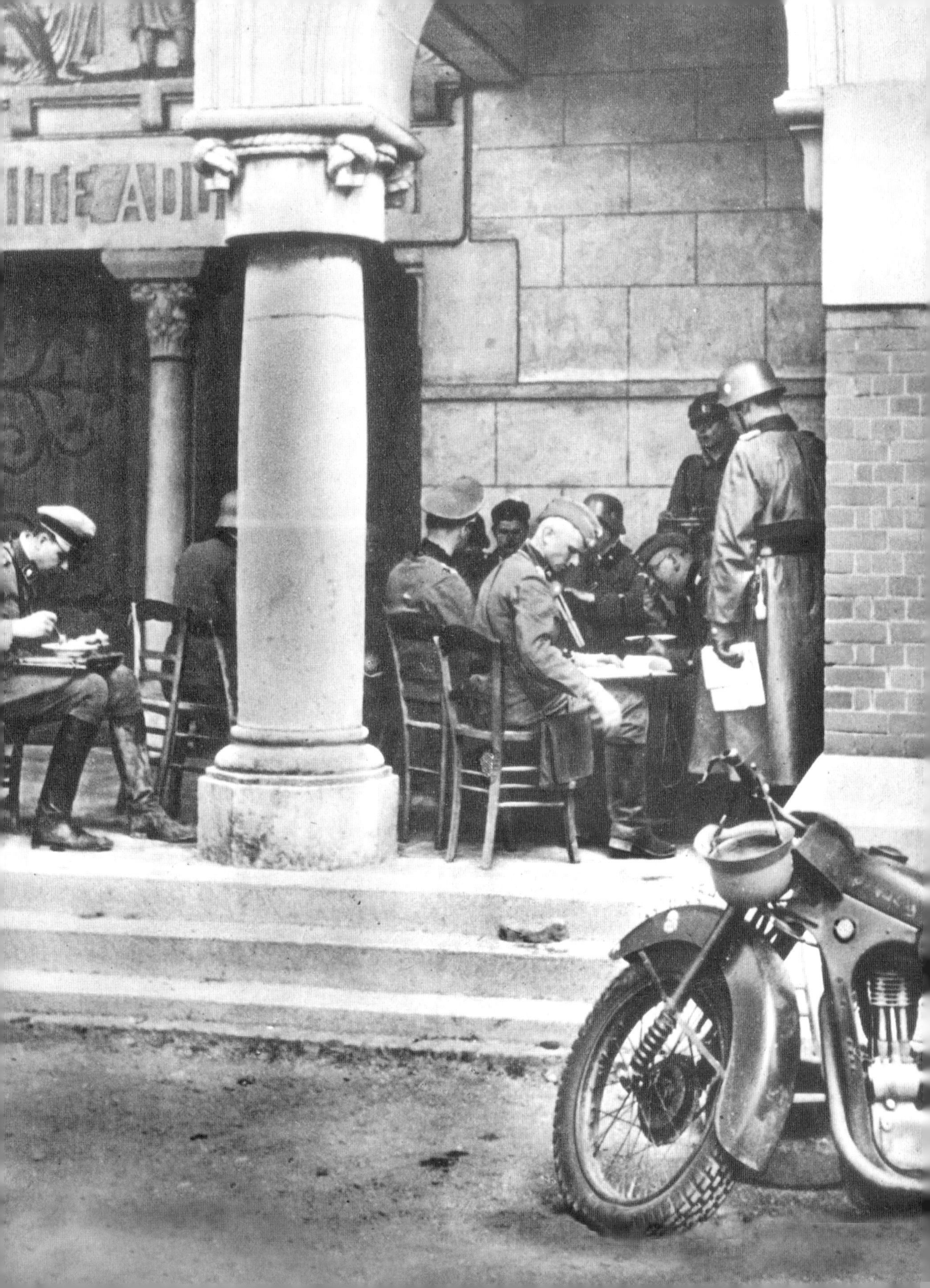

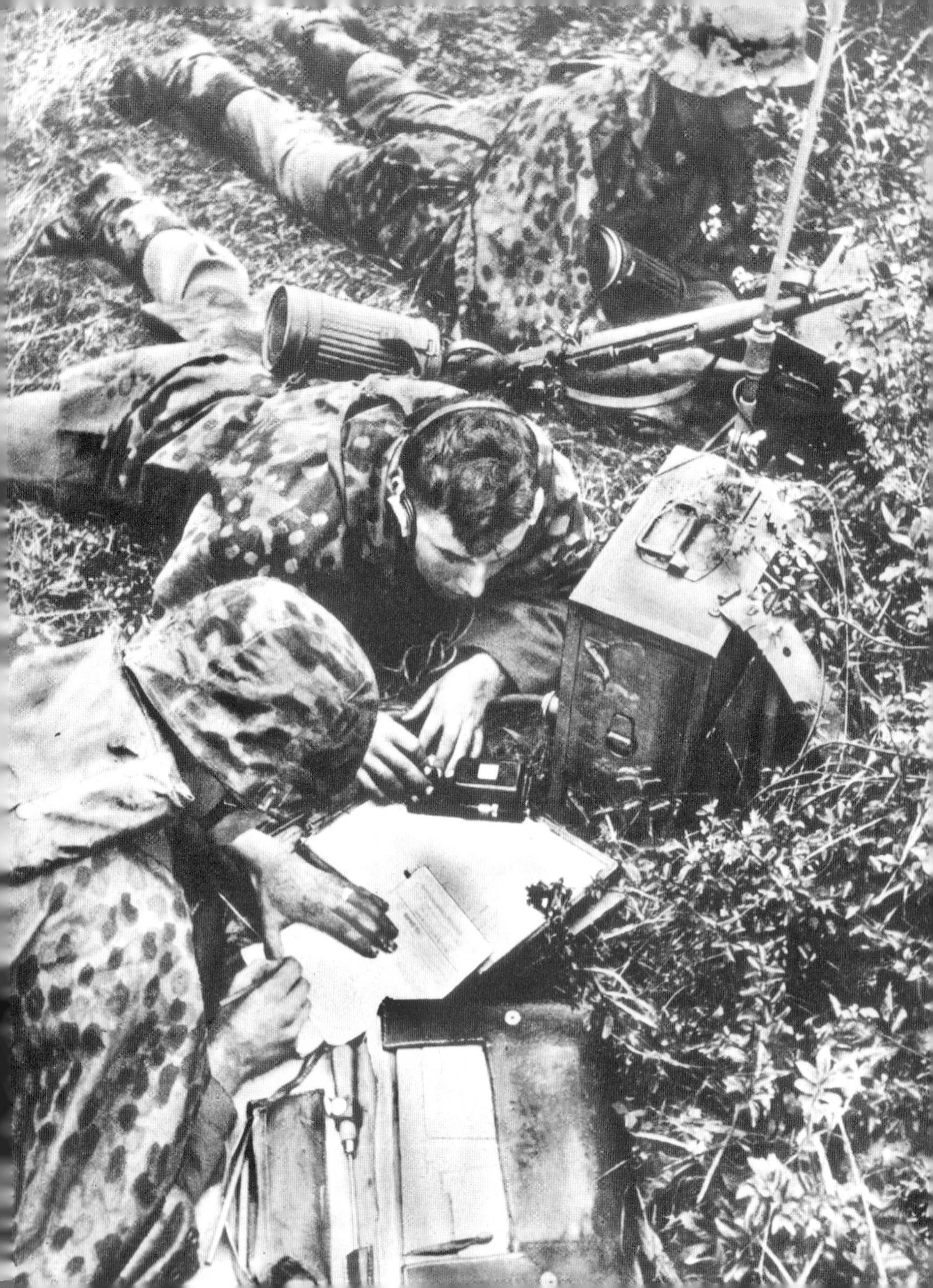

Four of our non-commissioned officers busy themselves with maps. Their work is demanding as they have to supply a constant flow of maps to the units at the point of the advance. The faster a fighting force advances, the larger will also be the demand for plans of the terrain. SSTrps64

The photographer put a storyline together showing how this mobile map unit supplied up-to-date mapping for the rapidly advancing *Totenkopf* Division...

Opposite and the original caption runs: *'What value do you put on the work we do?' is the question the operators ask us and we answer our comrades with the words 'You are the bond that holds together many of our combat units involved in this campaign.'* SSTrps61

In the middle of the advance are the motorcyclists; here one roars alongside the moving map wagon to pick up and deliver a map to a unit at the front awaiting its reception.
The truck is a converted civilian vehicle, Mercedes-Benz 4 × 2, belonging to Battalion HQ. SSTrps65

Opposite: *Despatch rider, after a dangerous ride, hands over the new maps to the leader of a reconnaissance unit and discusses the situation with him. At high speed our troops are advancing across a wide front.*
The armoured car is a Sd Kfz 222 (Gerät 81) which carried a crew of three. SSTrps66

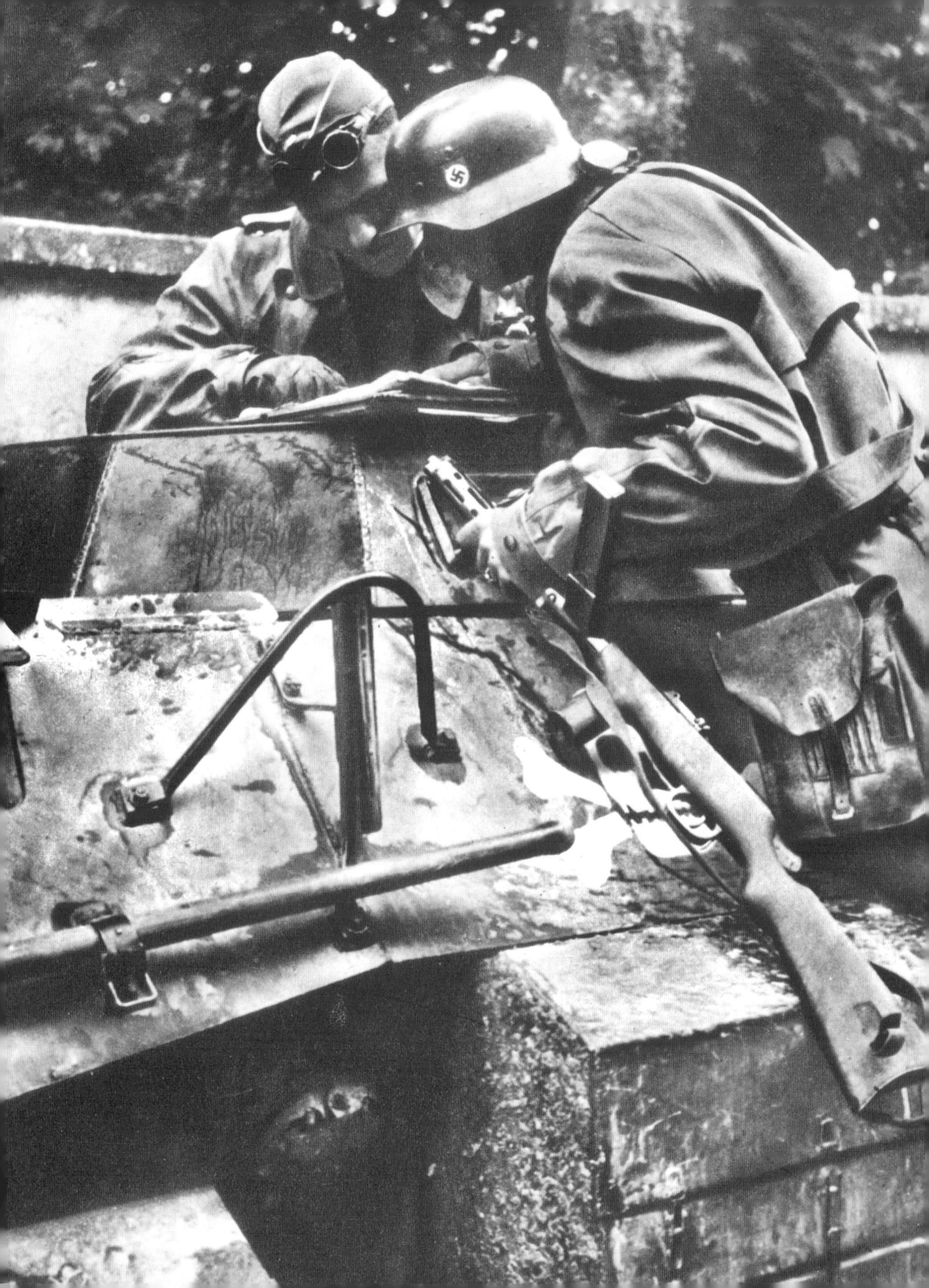

Right: A French Panhard P-178 armoured car with a dead crewman in the road. Captured vehicles were given German markings and pressed into service immediately. Around 350 of this type were in use by the French and a large number were captured in good condition. TLWW2ArmCar001

Below: A captured French P-178 bearing the *Totenkopf* insignia and German cross, advancing under fire along with supporting SS troops in leather coats. The original caption reads: *Forward! Hurry! In rapid foray our forward units advance against the many villages. The advance teams pave the way for the subsequent larger units which are coming up fast.* SSTrps68

A barricade across track blocks the way and our SS troops have taken cover. The obstacle receives a few grenades and black smoke still hangs over it. Our men, with a quick charge on the barricade, tear the obstruction aside. The way is open.   SSTrps67 and SSTrps69

The village must be clear of defenders as these *Totenkopf* troops have slung their rifles as they clear away another barricade at the far end of the village. SSTrps70

Chapter Five

Totenkopf – Engineers and Support Troops

THEY FIRED OTHER WEAPONS: *their job was to act as mediators between our fighting soldiers and the homeland. In words and pictures, in music and film, they brought home the news of the deeds of men who were fighting deep in enemy territory. It was not always easy, because instead of firing back to defend themselves, they could only push a camera button and report on the experiences of others. After several days of lively operations they finally fell back and were allowed to rest their dead-tired bones. However, even then it was most certainly no leisure time but rather they were engaged in typing up their stories – despite their heavy eyelids. And*

TLWW2Camera001   TLWW2Camera002

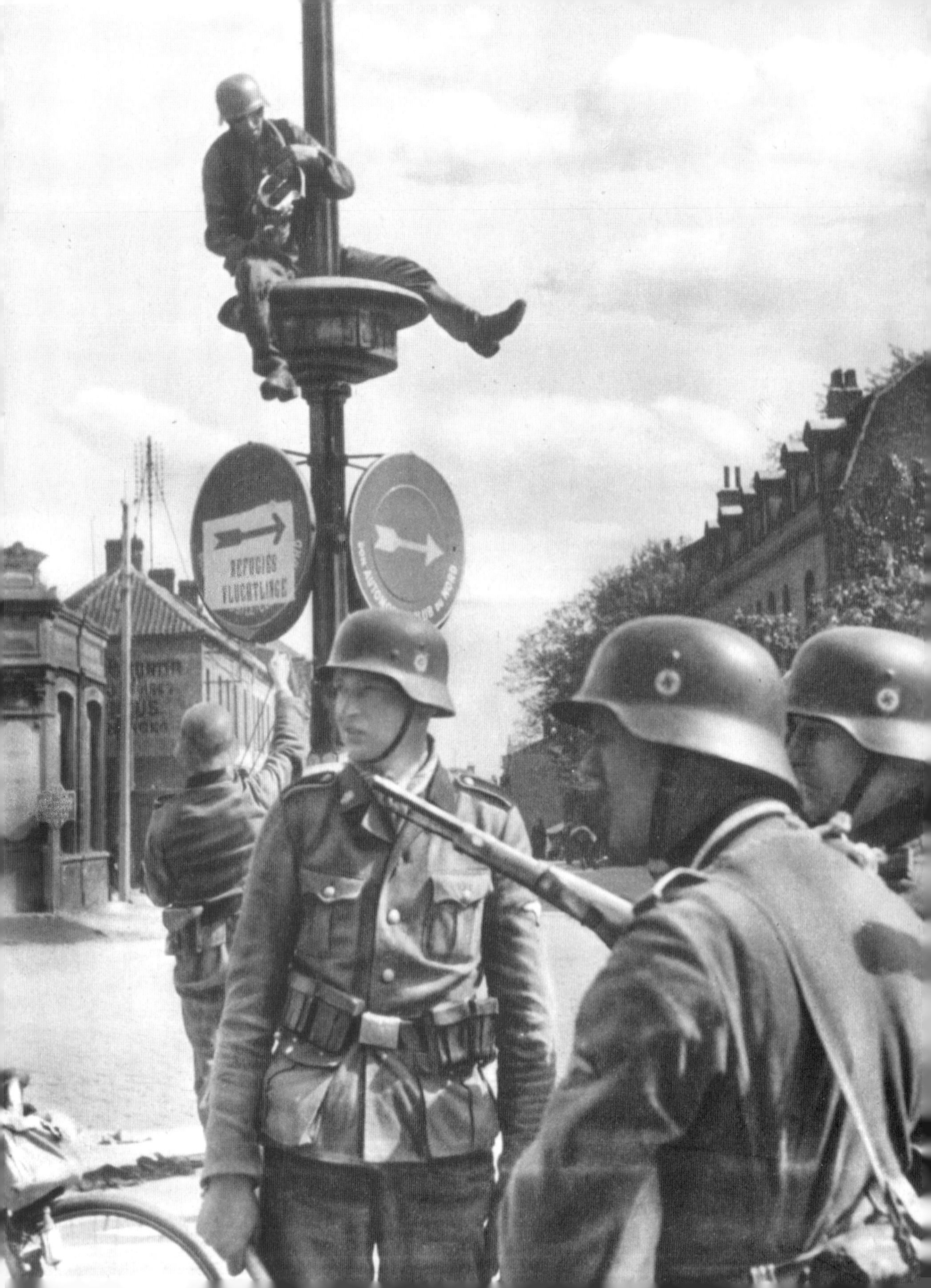
REFUGIES
FLUCHTLINGE

yet, it was done, it had to be done. They have learned their trade very quickly, through constant use of their 'other weapons'. All our war correspondents' reports by means of word and images, in film and sound, show how very soon, the fighting will be over as they conscientiously carry out their duties as mediators between the fighting front and the homeland.

The story of the part *Totenkopf* played in the invasion of the Low Countries, as told by its official war correspondents, takes a brief look at the work of the Division's engineers and other support troops introducing the subject by the following eulogy of their work in support of the front-line troops.

Comrades without glory

They, the silent unnamed and unknown to all their comrades worked with unselfish devotion to duty at their business. Your work will never be forgotten. Many of them most certainly would rather be where the action is but have eventually come to terms with the very different 'weapons' they have been called upon to use. Orders were orders and those with a greater insight than theirs made the assignments to a non combatant role and soon they could see how vital their work was in supporting their comrades who were fighting the enemy. In the field it was very hot and hard work with the bakers at their ovens, and the butchers having to work quickly do their work to ensure the troops were catered for. Like clockwork the support services knew that their efficiency had a part to play in the operational readiness of the soldiers. How much sweat ran down the foreheads and necks of our comrades in the repair shops of the maintenance units. Should any one of these support services fail then the Division would suffer. Our success depended upon them all and they have never let us down, these quiet, dutiful supporters of our Division.

One of the war correspondents accompanying the *Totenkopf* Division composed a poem to accompany and act as a caption to the photograph of a boyish looking despatch rider seated at the keys of a debris-strewn piano. The poetic rhetoric is styled to move the German readers to feelings of extreme national pride. Over the page. SSTrps33

Opposite: SS men of the War Correspondents Company and field police at a road junction in a French town. The photographer up the sign post is preparing to film an event during the advance deep into France. SSTrps32

That these hands – with which firm grip
Spanned minutes before the rifle
Braving all the bullets
The motorcycle ridden many days
Now, at last relaxed after activity of war,
Inspired by prayer – rest upon the keys.
Dedicated unto you **my comrades!**

And silence was come into your circle
And your eyes were misted over, as
Turning to the debris-laden piano,
From the very quietest in rippling chords

A Strauss waltz was heard – our master,
Was not home away in a far off land?
You felt moved **my comrades!**

The noise of battle could be heard,
Hammered out by the guns still yet.
Likely you would prefer a song of victory?
Which words would bear witness to your deeds
Death is conquered – your deeds live on
Then it is 'Yes' to life, to immortality
For Germany, **my comrades!**

FRITZ GERLACH

Opposite and we are informed: *No batch of meat will be issued to the troops, which has not been previously inspected very carefully with the microscope.* SSTrps51

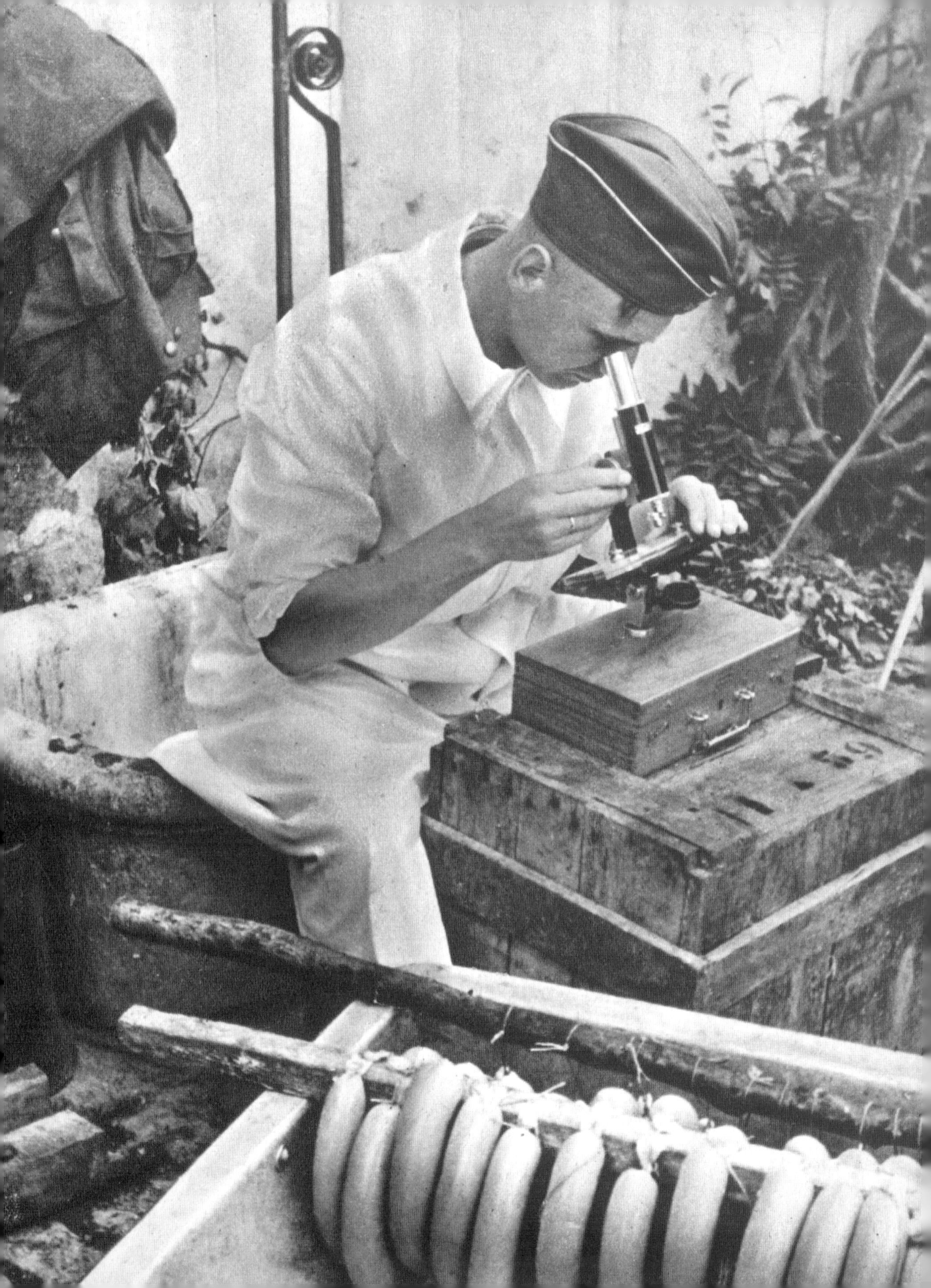

The 'breadbasket' of our division is just a part of the excellent organization of our mobile catering unit. 'I quietly do my duty here on behalf of my comrades and thereby have a part in the victories of our troops.' SSTrps52

Our 'bread-craftsmen' work tirelessly to provide for our appetites. Without reaping glory, these comrades are doing their hot service. We are indebted to them. SSTrps53

Stacks of newly baked bread. A 'munitions depot' for to our insatiable stomachs and just as important as bombs and bullets. This will allow our officers the necessary subsistence rations of bread for distribution to the men under their command. SSTrps54

A mobile workshop: a man works at on anvil. In a conscientious tireless work the men of the 'I-cars' ensure that our divisional vehicles remain serviceable for our forward-storming advance.

Opposite: An anti-tank gun covers engineers working on constructing a bridge across the La Bassée Canal. The workers seem unconcerned about the possibilities of an attack. Soon fire would come from the direction of Robecq and things would quickly change. SSTrps41

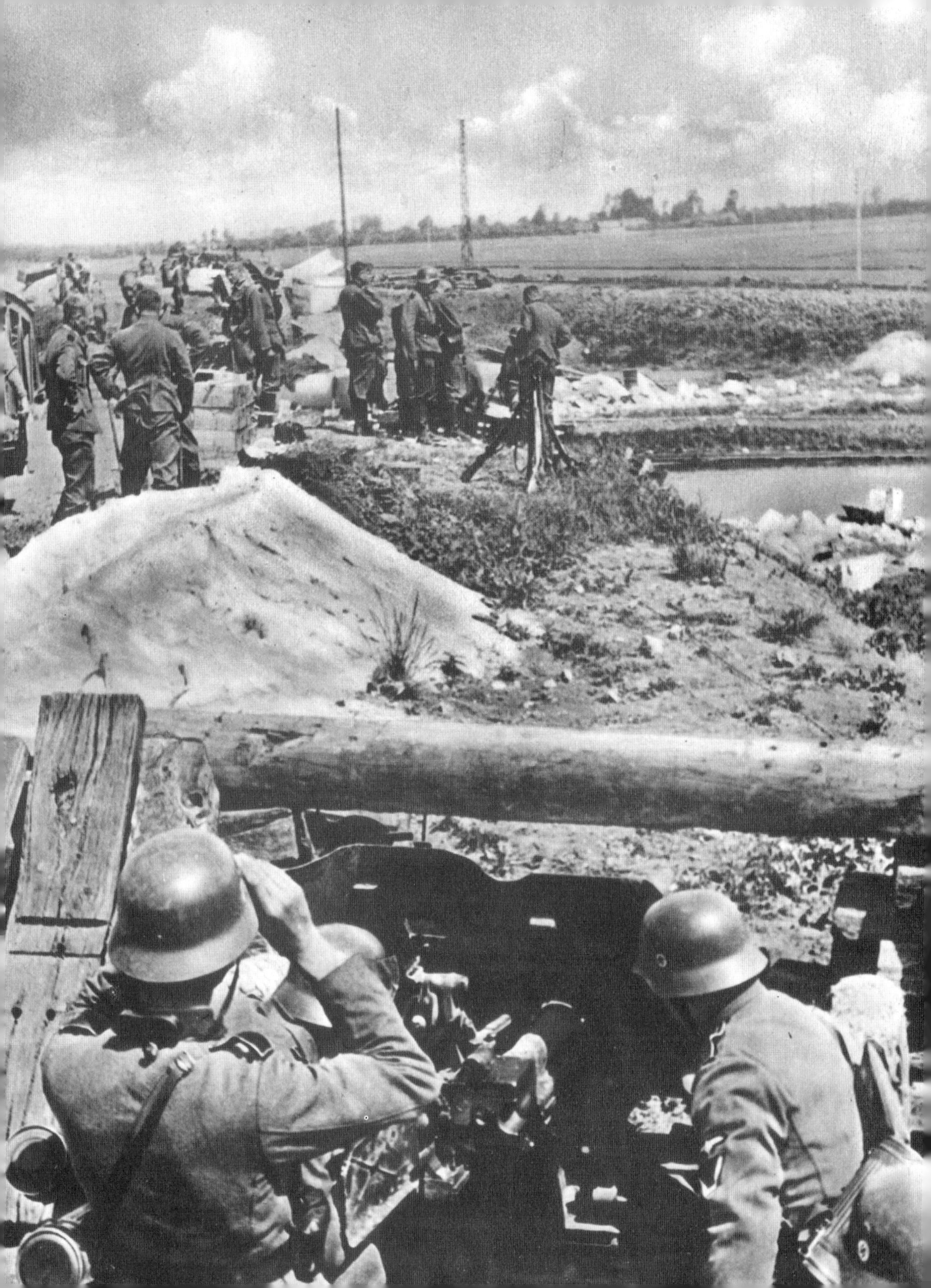

NCO with notebook details the jobs to be done to hooded men who have donned sacks as a cover from the rain. SSTrps43

In spite of bullets beginning to whistle around them our SS pioneers calmly repair a bridge demolished by the Tommies. Briefly they had to call a halt to their work but then carried on building again a little later. SSTrps42

Using a chain saw to put the finishing touches on this repaired bridge. Pride in their work causes our pioneers to do a neat job. SSTrps45

First lorry to drive over the recently repaired bridge. The last planks were are hardly laid as the first wagon of the column rolled across.
The lorry has the markings of a Totenkopf mortorized infantry unit. This is a 4 x 2 Adler light truck and may be a commandered civilian vehicle. SSTrps44

Chapter Six

Le Paradis – Atrocity against the Norfolks

SHE IS A VERY MUCH A 'MOBILE UNIT', our SS Totenkopf Division. For a motorized division speed means everything. We proved to be unpredictable for our opponents, fierce in the attack, unstopable, agile and fast in both the assault and in the pursuit. Whichever particular arm, infantry, artillery, Pak, signal troops or pioneers, they all acted like cogs in a great machine making up the Division driving westward. All worked closely together despite the unprecedented speed at which individual actions were fought. With our unstoppable speed, we overran and destroyed the defensive positions of the enemy. With our sheer pace we wore down the resolve of the opposition. Whether those staffing our mapping unit, or field kitchen, or whether those in our command headquarters or down to the least of the division's dispatch riders, everyone kept up a grinding pace. Courage, strength and dedication to the reputation we were acquiring, our men demonstrated these soldierly virtues which brought us the speedy victory.

Immense pride in themselves and their undoubted military expertise is seen throughout the book about the *Totenkopf* and its first action in France. The above is yet another example of the way they wished others to see them and just how they perceived themselves. Himmler's alternative formations to the German Army were in their infancy and were being forged in battle, therefore it was important to them that their accomplishments be brought to the attention of the German people. There were, however, some particular despicable events that the Division hoped would never become a part of public knowledge. Both *Waffen* SS divisions *Liebstandarte Adolf Hitler* and *Totenkopf* would carry out murders of surrendered British and French prisoners. The *Liebstandarte* confined eighty men of the Warwickshire Regiment in a barn and threw in grenades; any wounded survivors were then shot. There was just one survivor from the Royal Warwicks, Private Bert Evans, who managed to hide under the waters of a nearby pond. At that time members of the Cheshire Regiment and some French soldiers were also executed following their surrender to the *Liebstandarte*. Attempts in post-war years to bring the then commander of the *2.battalion Liebstandarte*, *SS-Hauptsturmführer* (Captain) Wilhelm Mohnke, to answer for the crime failed and Mohnke died at his home near Hamburg in 2001 aged ninety.

Le Paradis

Because of the attack by the British armour against the right flank of the panzer corridor thrusting towards the Channel, Hitler and the German High Command – *Oberkommando der Wehrmacht* (OKW) – ordered an all-out attack against the British troops forming a perimeter south of Dunkirk. On 24 May three SS divisions, SS-*Verfugungs*, SS-*Liebstandarte* and SS-*Totenkopf* were committed to this operation. On the sector the *Totenkopf* was earmarked to attack there were two water barriers, upper reaches of the Lys River and the La Bassée Canal and both crossings were hotly contested, especially by the Norfolks at La Bassée. Because of the determined defence of the British there were high casualties suffered by the attackers on Monday 27 May when a crossing was made at Béthune. Once across they then pushed on towards Merville. Fighting was particularly fierce at a group of farms near the village of Le Paradis where the 2nd British Infantry Division had been ordered to fight to the last. In the British 2nd Division was the 2nd Battalion of the Norfolks. Their

SS-*Hauptsturmführer* Wilhelm Mohnke (seen here with the rank of SS Colonel) commanded *2.battalion Liebstandarte Adolf Hitler*. He was unpopular with both his superiors and his subordinates who considered him to be brutal. He completed his wartime service with the rank of *Brigadeführer* commanding a last-ditch action in Berlin charged with Hitler's defence.

On the approaches to Le Paradis these men of SS-*Totenkopf* have pressed this French Somua S-35 into service painting the death's head badge and crosses on the turret and hull. TLWW2SSChar001

Over there, on the other side of La Bassée Canal, in the burning village of Robecq sits the British Tommy. A German tank probes the British forward defence perimeter.
SSTrps20

Once we have drained enough petrol from the sunken barges our pioneers can use such coal and petrol transporters as cover and as bridges to get across. Our men take cover from the firing coming from the beleaguered Tommies.

Does the original caption writer mean that the barges are filled with fuel and emptying them would cause the vessels to rise in the water, thus providing a means of cover from rifle and machine-gun fire coming from the houses? Perhaps, but it does give us a clear indication of just how close men of the SS War Correspondents Company were to the action. SSTrps21

Battalion War Diary reports the situation as it reached critical for them on Sunday 26 May 1940:

> During the night B and C Coys had moved to their correct positions and were dug in by first light. B Coy on the right of A Coy. At 03.00 hours the enemy made a determined attack on B Coy position and a lighter attack against C Coy on the

left flank. Enemy mortar fire was extremely accurate and caused heavy casualties. Fighting in the streets of the village and several local counter-attacks by B Coy assisted by 1st Royal Scots failed to restore the position completely and the general situation remained obscure. In the early morning both A and B Coys reported that they had been badly mauled and had hardly any men left. Captains Hastings and Long were sent to reorganize the survivors and make one unit of them. This was done successfully and about sixty men continued to fight in the Petit Cornet Malo area. Lieutenant Edgeworth was reported killed and this left no officer with B Coy. Casualties were growing in all companies and by early afternoon things were becoming desperate. Orders were received to hold the position until the last round and the last man.

Some personal experiences of the fighting from the defenders' point of view have been recorded by author historian Peter Hart and can be found in his book *The 2nd Norfolk Battalion – From Le Paradis to Kohima* published by Pen & Sword in 2011 in their paperback series *Voices from the Front*. This is an extract quoting the experiences of Private Ernie Farrow, Pioneer Section HQ Coy, 2nd Norfolks:

We had to go between two different companies – just the Pioneers which was about twenty of us because we'd lost about eight men by this time. What they told us to do was to go up on to the top of this canal bank and make sure that every round that we fired got a German. We were getting short of ammunition and we must try and make every round count. I was using my .303 rifle. Occasionally we took turns in firing the Bren gun but there again we had to be very careful. We found that by using the rifles we could save quite a lot of ammunition. We could pick a German off with our rifle just as well as we could do with the Bren gun where you'd fire probably twenty rounds ten hit the same

British Tommies in their fox holes on a defence line leading to the Dunkirk perimeter. TLWW2BEF001

His every move observed the enemy was pinned to the ground as the loud chatter of our machine gun delivered aimed, deliberate bursts of fire.

Made in Czechoslovakia, this 7.92 mm machine gun, model 37, was used by German forces throughout the Second World War. Also manufactured in Britain and known as the BESA and used by the British army. SSTrps22

Crossing a canal with efficiency and speed. With a few quick jumps, the pioneers of the SS are out of their cover and already at the canal; quickly they slide the rubber boat into the water. SSTrps25

Over the canal and attacking over open fields towards the village where they have been holding us up for the last few days. Then we drove him back in retreat. SSTrps24

For the defending British Bren gun teams there was no shortage of tagets – just a shortage of ammunition. BEF2

German. After we'd fired a certain amount of rounds, we'd got to scramble back down the bank of the canal, run along a bit, then go up top again just to try and bluff the Germans that there was a great company of us there. We were being hard pressed, we were being machine gunned, mortared, shelled.

We had been led to believe that the

Crossing the canal under cover of smoke screen. *Under cover of heavy support weapons our men paddle their Pak over the canal. One after another the boats begin crossing and the bridgehead is formed.* SSTrps21

'Where did that shot come from?' A British sniper finds his target and the SS adjutant is killed outright. A *Waffen* SS cameraman is on hand to capture the dramatic action as it happens.
TLWW2Sniper001 TLWW2Sniper002

German tanks were made of cardboard and plywood but by God we knew the difference when they started firing at us – we got our heads down very, very quickly! The most terrible thing that I've ever experienced. We were dug in our little fox holes and we'd keep our heads down but you couldn't be there all the time – you had to get up to fire at the Germans on the other side because those Germans were trying to get across

85

The heavy mortars are to give support for our infantry providing the necessary fire power to suppress the enemy. They are using an 8 cm schwere Granatwerfer 34. This heavy support weapon was brought into service in 1934 and saw service throughout the war. SSTrps28

the canal to get at us! The more we were hiding up the less chance we had of stopping them. So we had to go out and fire at them. They were even driving their lorries into the canal and trying to drive their tanks across on these lorries. But the artillery managed to keep them at bay. I don't think we saw an aircraft over our sector at the time.

Headquarters Company of the 2nd Norfolks holding out in farm buildings at Druries Farm were almost out of ammunition and were cut off. The Germans were across the canal in strength and the situation for the Norfolks became hopeless. The British officer went around the beleaguered defenders asking them if they were for surrendering or fighting on. Some were in high spirits despite the desperate position and pointed out that they were still causing heavy casualties among the attackers and should fight on. The officer, Major Ryder, pointed out that they had held the Germans up for three days on the canal but could not hope to hold out indefinitely, that it was pointless wasting human lives. A white towel was attached to a rifle and waved, then men walked out behind it their hands in the air. The Norfolks had

An overturned burning car provides cover against machine-gun fire zipping across the flat road. With one mighty leap, the squad overcome this dangerous road.

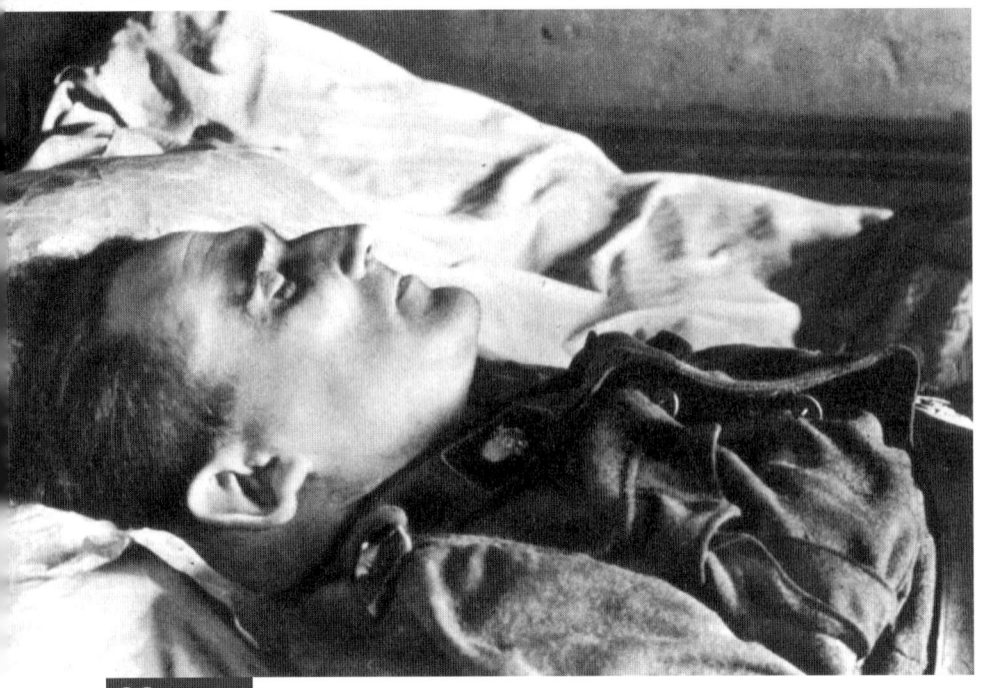

Searching through the buildings of a captured farm. The oblong canvas bag on the chest contains an anti-gas cape which item of equipment was never used for what it was intended. It was eventually discarded along with the gasmask. TLWW2Sniper3003

Shot and killed by one of the Norfolks defending the La Bassée Canal, *Standartenführer* Hans Friedemann Götze, *Regimentskommandeur* in the *Totenkopf* Division, seen here prior to his burial, laid out in a French farmhouse near Le Paradis. SSTrps28

Two SS men pause during grave digging for one of their commrades on the banks of the canal. Awaiting temporary internment lies the body of a fellow SS soldier. Battalions of the British 2nd Infantry Division had put up a fierce defence and casualties had been high among the officers and men of *Totenkopf*.

'Ich hat einen Kameraden!'
'I once had a comrade!'

surrendered to SS troopers of *14.Kompanie, 1.Battalion, 2.Regimient SS-Totenkopfdivision* commanded by SS-*Hauptsturmführer* Fritz Knochlein.

The moment of surrender is always the most dangerous time for the defeated combatants; will the victors keep their fingers off their triggers? Will a nervous, traumatized soldier lose control and open fire on them? Once a surrender is accepted and prisoners gathered together for safe removal from the battle zone then the danger for them should be deemed to be over.

Not on this occasion for prisoners of the *Totenkopf*. Two machine guns from *4.Maschinengewehrkompanie* were set up by a barn in a paddock of Creton Farm. The prisoners were marched down the road from

89

SS-*Hauptsturmführer* Fritz Knochlein commanding 14.Kompanie, 1.Battalion, 2.Regiment SS-Totenkopfdivision. This photograph of Knochlein was taken a few days after the massacre. FitzKnochlein

The photograph below was taken by a German soldier the day after the attrocity and before the bodies of the slain Norfolks were buried.

where they had been captured at Duries Farm and through a gate into a field and lined up against the wall. The two machine gunners opened fire and continued firing until all were down. Knöchlein then ordered his men to fix bayonets and finish off any still left alive. Satisfied that they had killed them all, the German SS men left to rejoin the continuing advance. A surviving victim tells the story:

> There were a hundred of us prisoners marching in column of threes. We turned off the dusty French road through a gateway and

For what are you fallen? The medical orderly came too late. They died for England. British Tommies lie where they were killed in the heat of battle on the banks of the La Bassée Canal defending the way to Dunkirk. SSTrps31

into a meadow beside the buildings of a farm. I saw, with one of the nastiest feelings I've ever had in my life, two heavy machine guns inside the meadow. They were manned and pointing at the head of our column. I felt as though an icy hand gripped my stomach. The guns began to spit fire and even as the front men began to fall I said fiercely, 'This can't be. They can't do this to us!' For a few seconds the cries and shrieks of our stricken men drowned the cracking of the guns. Men fell like grass before a scythe. The invisible blade came nearer and then swept through me. I felt a terrific searing pain in my left leg and wrist and pitched forward in a red world of tearing agony. My

Fresh from the fight, covered with mud and with signs of the hard struggle they have just experienced on their faces. Clearly their expressions show their relief to be alive.
SSTrps35

A captured British Tommy at headquarters waiting to be questioned.
TLWW2Britpris001

scream of pain mingled with the cries of my mates but even as I fell forward into a heap of dying men the thought stabbed my brain, 'If I ever get out of here the swine who did this will pay for it'.

Signaller Albert Pooley, A Coy, 2nd Norfolks

Ninety-seven British prisoners were killed and next day the Germans enlisted locals to bury the bodies in a shallow mass grave, but not before a number of German officers and a German journalist had visited the scene. Gunter d'Alquen was a member of the SS War Correspondents, who arrived at the farm with Dr Thum, the *Totenkopf* deputy legal advisor. Gunter d'Alquen made a report of what he saw:

> It was possible to look into the back yard from the road where the corpses in British uniform were lying in the yard near the buildings. They were lying in such a position that one can assume they were killed by machine-gun bursts. It struck me at once that the dead soldiers were not wearing helmets, nor did they have any equipment on them. I took pictures of the dead bodies, and the whole farm. Thum requested that these were to be placed at the disposal of the division. Major Friedkerr von Riedner, who was also at the scene of the massacre on that day, reported that, "These people had almost all suffered head wounds from shots that must have been fired at close range. Some had their whole skull smashed in, an injury that can almost only be caused by a blow from a gun butt or some such similar means."

Neighbouring German divisions soon became aware of the massacre and the news spread until eventually *Leutnantgeneral* Erich Höpner, commander of the German

These prisoners from the Royal Scots captured at the same time of the Le Paradis incident, could expect treatment as laid down for prisoners of war by the Geneva Convention which had entered into force in June 1931. It covered the treatment of prisoners of war during the Second World War.
TLWW2Scotspris001

forces in France got to hear of it. He disliked the SS, especially Eicke, and was determined to have him dismissed if charges of mistreatment or murdering of prisoners could be brought. However no meaningful investigation was undertaken as steps to do so were blocked by the SS, who did not consider the *Wehrmacht* sufficiently without bias to carry out an

Hopes of medical treatment and survival for prisoners was largely a matter of chance: wounded and falling prisoner to the *Totenkopf* (right) and wounded in the hands of the *Wehrmacht* (below). WW2BEFPris

SS-*Obergruppenführer* Josef 'Sepp' Dietrich. TLWW2Dietrich003

'Human life matters very little to the SS and will not interfere with the fulfillment of a mission' was the comment of SS-*Obergruppenführer* Josef 'Sepp' Dietrich, commander of the SS-*Liebstandarte*, when the matter of massacre of the Norfolks was under investigation by the *Wehrmacht. commander* General Höpner. It is reported that the remark incensed Höpner who considered Dietrich's comment to be irresponsible and he condemned the high casualties suffered by the *Waffen* SS in the fighting so far. He called Dietrich a butcher in front of his own officers.

Leutnantgeneral Erich Höpner, an officer of the old school, had problems coming to terms with the concept of a parallel army to the *Wehrmacht* the *Waffen* SS. Massacre of the Norfolks confirmed his concerns and he sought to have the commander of the *Totenkopf* dismissed.

investigation. Nevertheless, many SS officers themselves were appalled by the massacre; some reportedly even challenged Knöchlein to a duel. None were ever fought and the stain against the *Totenkopf* remained. Its reputation grew and darkened after the invasion of Soviet Russia in 1941.

Despite thorough efforts to exterminate all massacre victims Private William O'Callaghan had survived and he had located and pulled Private Albert Pooley alive from among the bodies in the field. The pair then hid in a pig-sty for three days and nights, surviving on raw potatoes before being discovered by the farm's owner. The two survivors, O'Callaghan and Pooley were later captured by the *251.Infantriedivision* – a *Wehrmacht* unit and passed safely into medical care and captivity.

Other prisoners captured at around the same time by the *Totenkopf* are also believed to have been murdered, including twenty men of the Royal Scots, a mass grave having been discovered in the area of Le Paradis in 2007.

Last goodbye – a few wild flowers, a bouquet from a cottage garden, a silent look, a short Message: 'I had a comrade'!
Men of the *Totenkopf* Division could and did show great sympathy for their own killed and wounded. SSTrps39

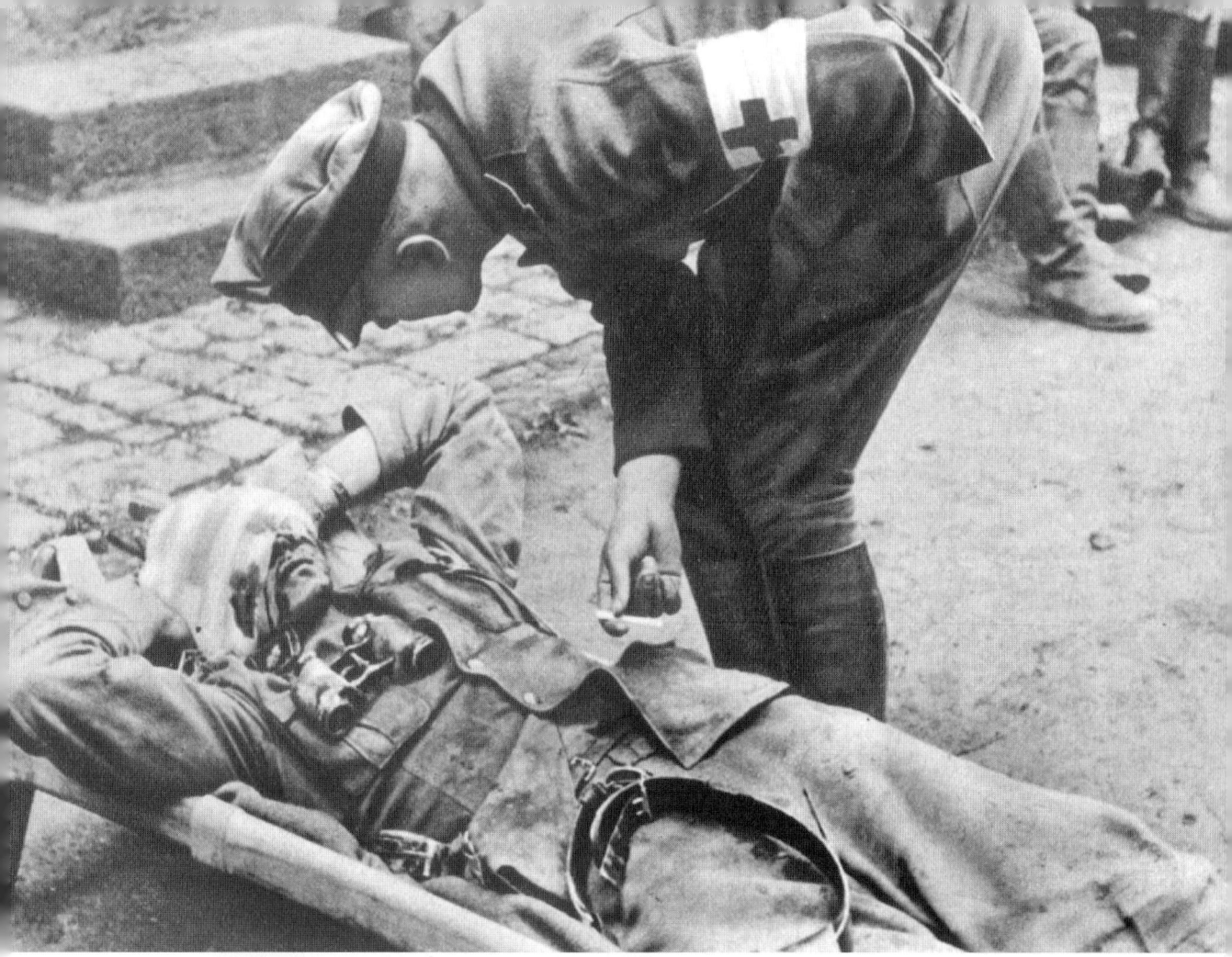

'Here is a cigarette, Komrade, not long to wait now – we are moving you to a hospital bed!' The medical orderly at the main dressing station offers to help him smoke a cigarette as he reassures the severely wounded Totenkopf officer.
SSTrps36

A severely wounded SS soldier is comforted by an orderly.
SSWounded005

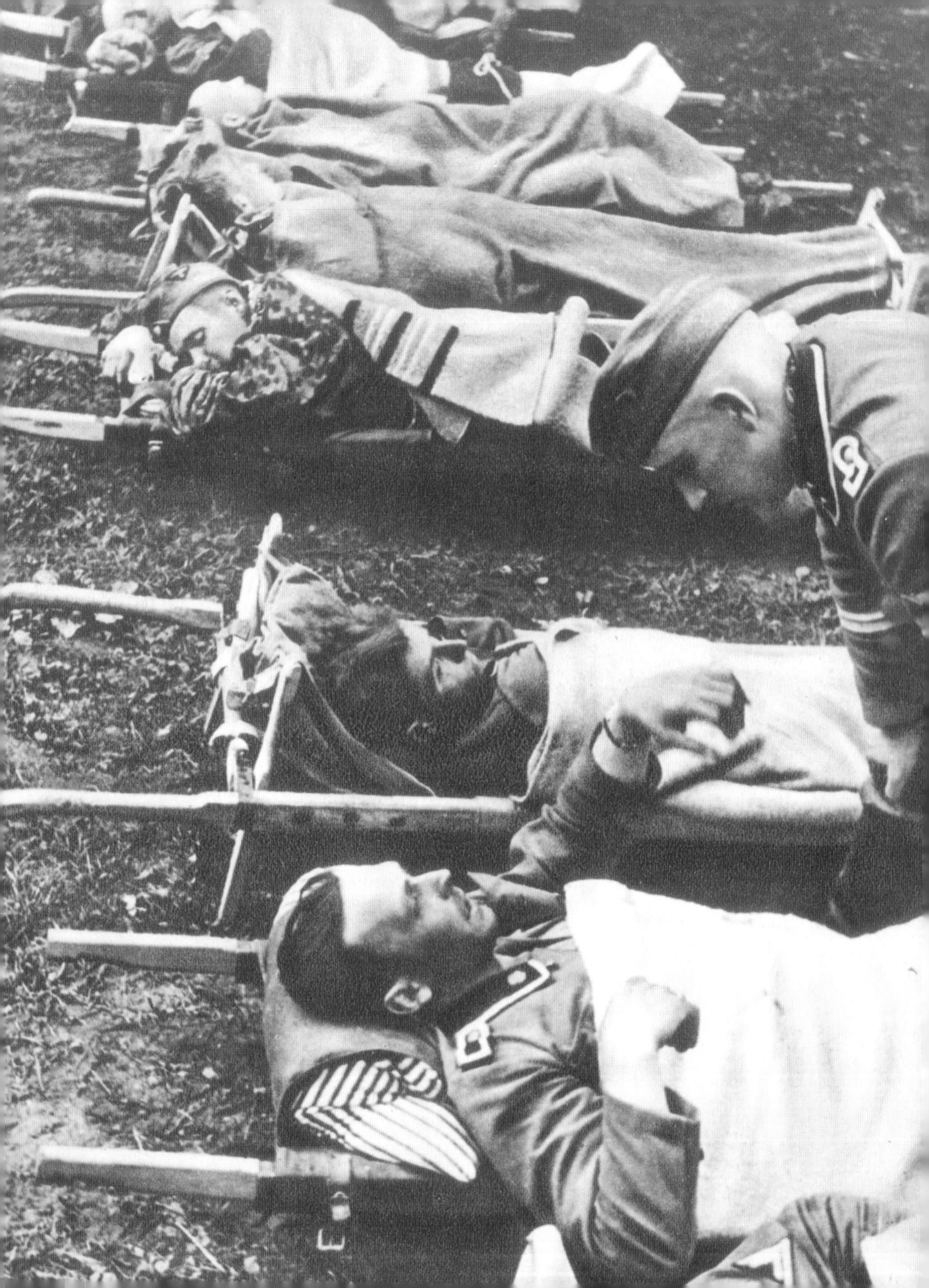

Simple crosses by the road; the helmets throw a gentle shadow on the names of the fallen. A group of SS men pass by for a final look before they march towards the enemy. They belive in the simple saying: 'One has flown, will you or I be the next to follow?' SSTrps40

Opposite: A line of stretcher cases and every man will be attended to. The surprising thing is that no one complains or groans. An NCO inquires of a severely wounded comrade. Sometimes it is as though we see a gentle smile as they visit our brave comrades. SSTrps37

From here, he has a good view.
Surveying the line of the continuing advance from the hull of an abandoned French R-35 light tank is this well equipped *Totenkopf* NCO.
SSTrps46

Chapter Seven

Approaches to the Channel Coast

LIKE A GIANT SPEAR thrusting through, German tanks and our fast motorized divisions lance through the front of our opponents. In the heady thrust we overrun Dutch, Belgian, French and Englishmen splitting the enemy's northern armies from those in the south. Roaring along we destroy each strongpoint in turn before rolling onwards – the SS-Totenkopf Division thunders inexorably along narrow roads south of Arras in hostile territory. It was only as they were being taken prisoner that our opponents suddenly seemed to recognize what was happening to them. By then it was already far too late.

They had played their last card when they attempted to counter-attack us at Arras and broke on the fierce resistance of the death's head. Our heavy weapons saved the day when SS-Totenkopf Division shattered the last hope of our enemies.

'A German lot? "Yes, well the desire of many Frenchmen for invasion and occupation was being fulfilled. Only they had imagined that the boot would be on the other foot and the tour would be in the opposite direction. SSTrps48

Men slept where and when there was a halt in the relentless drive towards the Channel Ports. Here an officer and his driver have succumbed in broad daylight to the overpowering need to sleep and have been captured on film. TLWW2SSsleep002

Below is a poem penned by a soldier of the *Waffen* SS and displayed on the walls of some SS barracks. Note the confident reference to divine support for their killing operations in the last line.

If one of us becomes tired
   The other watches for him –
If one of us has doubts,
   The other laughs reassuringly –
If one of us should fall,
   The other takes the place of two –
For God gives every warrior a comrade.
         Herybert Menzel (killed in action)

Opposite: SS Motorcycle troops exhausted and asleep sat up. Motorized infantry when dismounted seek rest, where and how become secondary. They sleep in the saddle, lying down, squatting or sitting and if need be – standing up! SSTrps34

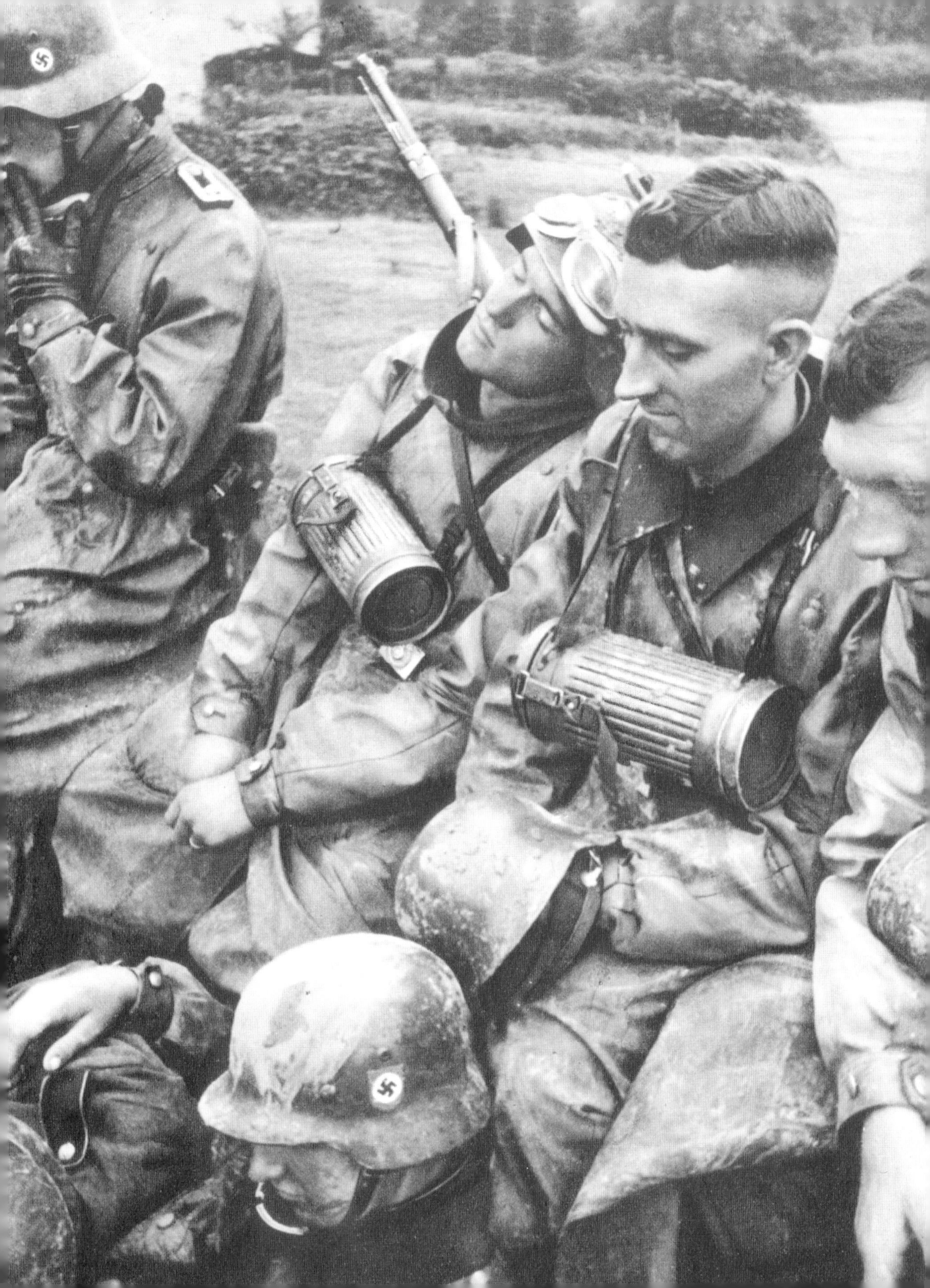

Lying on top of banking observing. A commander takes a look for himself.
Note the motorcycle combination in the background – likely the means of transport for this SS officer and his aide engaged in observing the way ahead. SSTrps56

Opposite: French prisoners of the *Totenkopf* having their possesions searched. One of the prisoners appears to be wearing civilian clothes and looks worried – with good reason. Should he be judged to be a *franc-tireurs*, civilian sniper, he will be shot out of hand. The other two prisoners appear less concerned.
Prisoner control – their packs and identification papers are examined by our SS comrades. SSTrps47

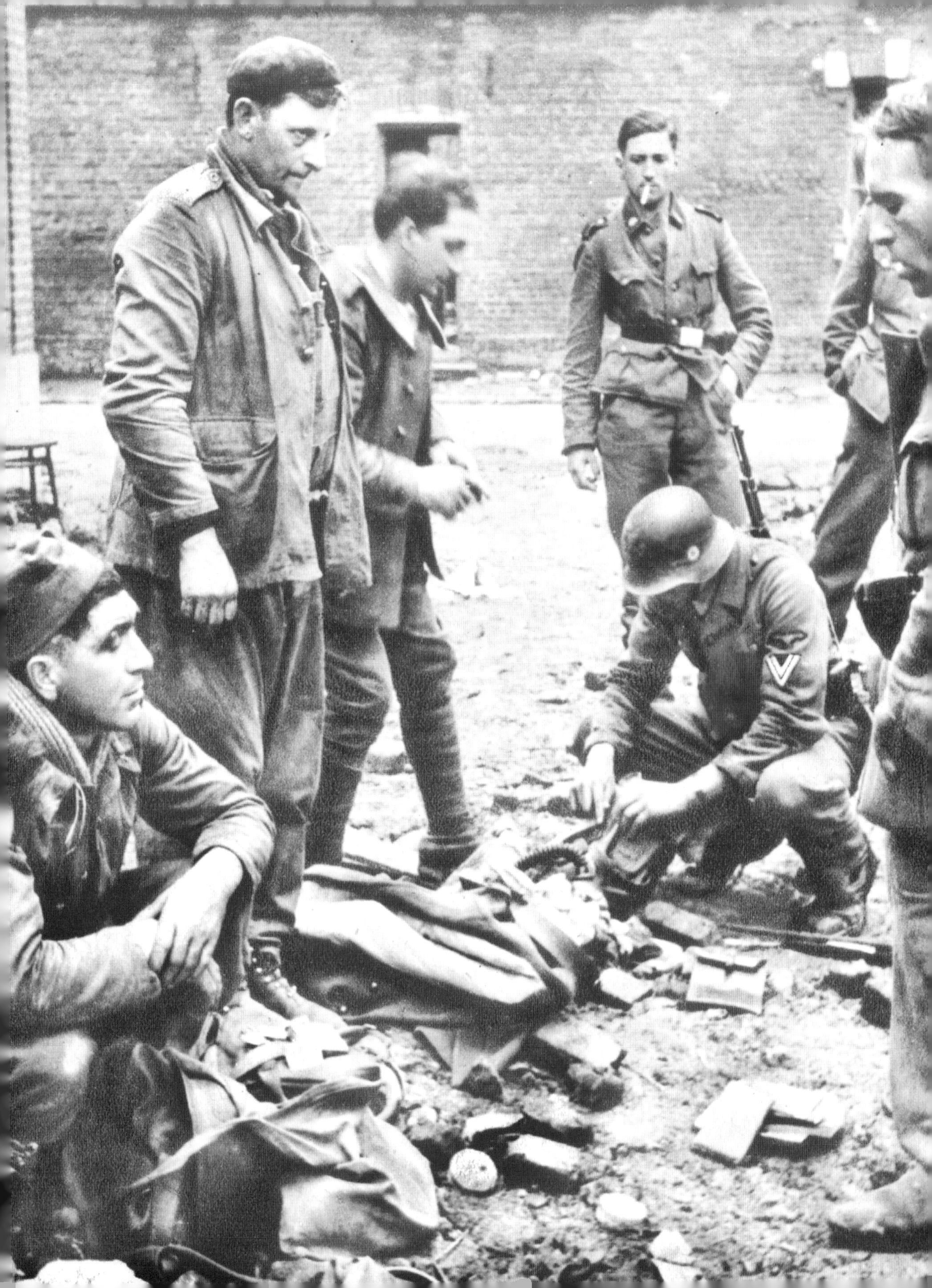

During our advance we captured immense quantities of ammunition at road-side dumps, which were originally intended as love gifts for us but they never reached their intended target.
A *Totenkopf* artillery NCO examines the fuses at this supply dump storing shells for a French 194 mm *Grand Puissance Filloux* gun (gun of great power). SSTrps49

A French aircraft hanger after a visit by Stuka diver bombers.
Left: *A huge French 'Transporter' was destroyed on the ground. It was used by our comrades as a temporary shelter. It appears to be a French Bloch MB-131 bomber.* SSTrps50

Road north-west of Arras busy with military traffic. The private car belonging to a *Totenkopf* motorized unit bears the divisional skull badge. The armoured car is a Sd Kfz 232. TLWW2SSCar001

The British are in headlong flight in the direction of Dunkirk. In a wild chase, we are after them until we reach Bailleul. The staff car with the officer reading a map is a 4x4 vehicle, Kfz15, built by AU/Horch and Opel EFm. SSTrps79

Our Stukas had trapped the Tommies in Bailleul. Wreckage of the British Expeditionary Force blocked just about every street in the city. SSTrps80

Bailleul suffers the ravages of war once more and this time it is razed to the ground. Following the First World War the damage was repaired, funded by German war reparations. SSTrps81

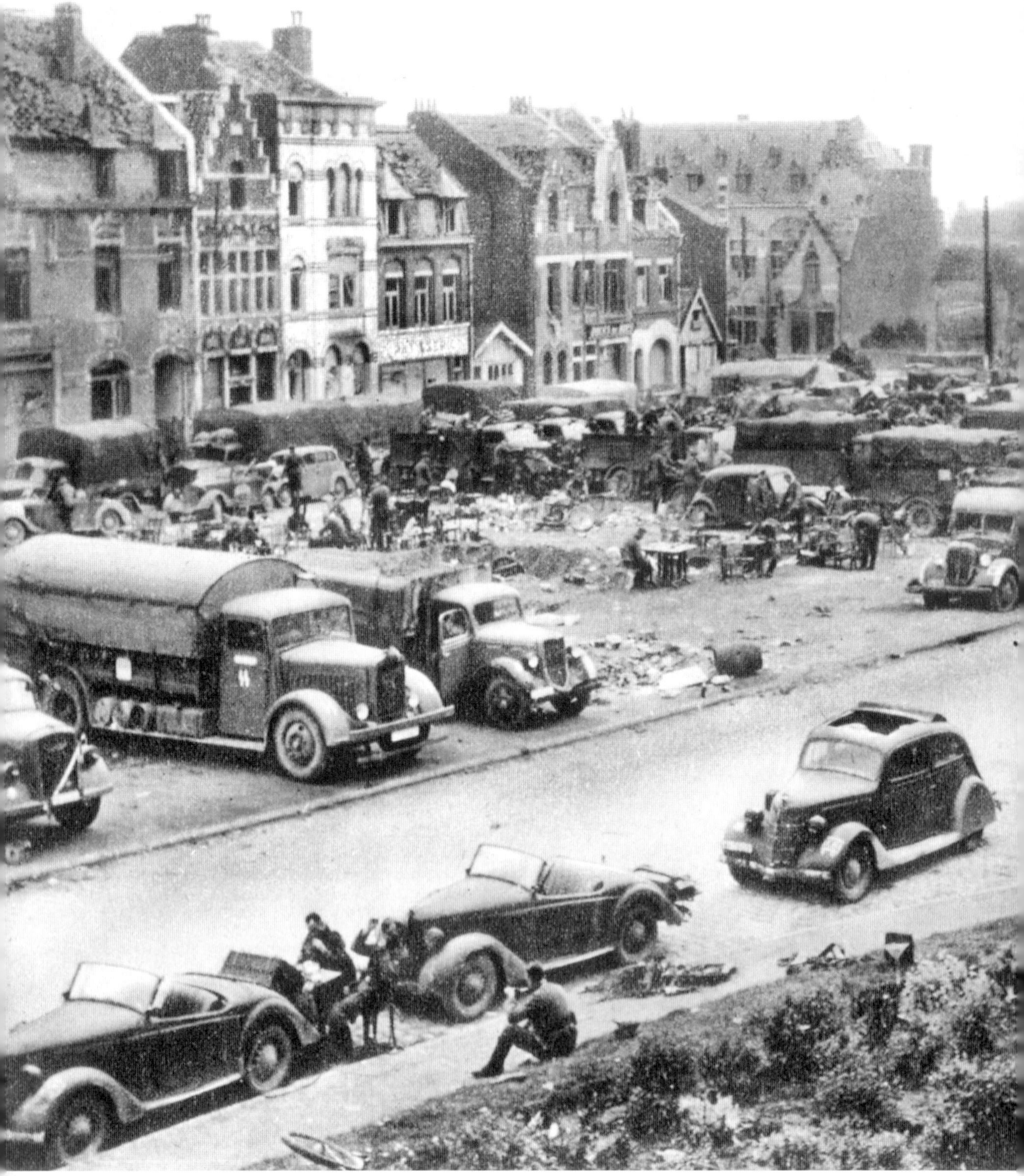

Men of the Waffen SS laid French soldiers in their final resting place.

Left: Our columns of wagons parked on the square at Bailleul. Our men are enjoying a meal surrounded by rubble. Once again the burning brand of war strikes this town. However, the fault is of their own making they were the ones who brought down evil upon Bailleul. SSTrps82

Below: Bailleull in 1918 – a scene of total devastation. The original English caption reads: 'Condition of the town when the invader left it, never to return, 30 August 1918.' Twenty-two years later the invader did returned and, on this occasion, blamed the French themselves for the resulting damage.

The *Totenkopf* parade in front of the Cafe Bellevue. *Our comrades gather outside the Town Hall shortly after the capture of Bailleul, the occasion is the award of decorations.* SSTrps83

'*For bravery in the face of the enemy!* "*The group leader* [Scharführer], *of our artillery won his Iron Cross by directing fire at Le Paradise. Simple bravery was sufficient reward.*

One officer and four *Totenkopf* NCOs receive the Iron Cross; SS-*Obersturmführer* (lieutenant); SS-*Scharführer* (colour sergeant); SS-*Unterscharführer* (sergeant); SS-*Oberscharführer* (n/a); SS-*Sturmmann* (lance corporal). Two are wearing trade proficiency arm badges *Richtabzeichen für Artillerie-Richtkanonier* (Gun Layer, Artillery). SSTrps84

On the way to Boulogne sur Mer. In the small French town of Marquise these men in civilian clothes greeted our arrival with arms raised in salute, 'Heil Hitler!' they called to us. They were displaced Dutchman, Mussert-people who welcomed us with joy as liberators.
Mercedes-Benz lorry with British steel helmet hung on radiator as a trophy; also a British bayonet has been pushed through the Mercedes badge. This truck belongs to an anti-tank unit of SS-Totenkopf. SSTrps85

Chapter Eight

The Sea – A Goal Achieved

THE FIGHTING IN ARTOIS AND FLANDERS is behind us. In a quick drive we stormed to the sea. How hard was it once in the First World War as others fought for this same goal, the way to the sea? At that time it was to remained a goal which, despite the highest commitment, could not be reached. We experienced feelings of pride and a great

The *Waffen* SS divisions had proved their value by fighting to victory against the Allies alongside the German Army. Here a three-man crew man their Besa machine gun during the fighting in France.

comrade – what our fathers once aspired to, we had accomplished. We fought our way through to the sea, to the Channel.

By towering clouds, which stood above the water, the last rays of sunshine broke through and poured over the sea with a flood of light that looked like pure gold. Black and Blue was the silhouette of the wrecked steamer on the beach. Overcome with emotion at beauty of it all was an old comrade who had fought once before on the soil of Flanders but never did, of course, reach the beaches – the sea! How could anyone have ever imagined that one day the goal would be reached.

The beautiful days of Boulogne and that was followed by time spent further up the coast at Ambleteuse. They were days of rest, days of relaxation, enjoying the roaring of the waves of the enjoyable cooling effectup to the chest and shoulders in the sea. And over there we could see in the light of the setting sun – ENGLAND!

A monument to failure this French Char B1 lies abandoned, just one of hundreds scattered across the countryside on the approaches to Dunkirk and other Channel ports. 45Char002

An age-old occupation of the victors – they get to riffle through the baggage train.

The German cameramen have many photographic opportunities as columns of prisoners stream by and all manner of equipment is scattered about the streets. 84DUN012   74Negros001

They fought shoulder to shoulder, white and coloureds! – as comrades?
The German caption writer introduces disbelief when he questions the fact that French soldiers of mixed races could work together.
SSTrps91

So war das Ende! So was the end. SSTrps92

Betrayed and abandoned by their allies, march the soldiers of the 'Great Nation' into captivity. SSTrps90

They have met their match and these captured British have very quickly forgotten. their high-spirited song about 'hanging out their washing on the Siegfried Line'. SSTrps89

Pak takes up a defensive position on the Channel coast. SSTrps92

DE CRÊTE
A CRÊTE
DE VILLE
A VILLE
DE CONTINENT
A CONTINENT

Until such time as our comrades of the Marine Artillery arrived to take over, our men of the heavy artillery manned the shore batteries and commenced firing the large calibre guns at targets out to sea at once. Loud was the thunder from them which rolled across the sea to England. SSTrps88

Military equipment and supplies left behind by the British in their 'victorious retreat'.
The British truck is a Humber FWD 8-cwt 4 x 4 belonging to the Royal Artillery. They were rendered useless by draining the oil and running the engines until they seized up. 89Brittrucks11

This caption simply states: *At the Channel.* This had been the goal of the Germans in the Great War and some veterans of that conflict, arriving at the beaches, were emotionally affected. SSTrps86

Great memories of the SS Totenkopf Division during the French Campaign 1940

Appendices

D. S. 1 Dunkerque-Plage / Duinkerke-Strand 1940 Croiseur échoué. Gestrande Kruizer.

D. S. 2 Dunkerque-Plage / Duinkerke-Strand 1940 Croiseur échoué. Gestrande Kruiser.

D. S. 3 Dunkerque-Plage / Duinkerke-Strand 1940 Torpilleur échoué.

Part of a set of ten postcards German soldiers could send home to memorialise the speedy victory achieved against the Allies.

SS-Totenkopf Division
Order of battle (1940)

I.Regiment
II.Regiment
III.Regiment
Artilerie-Regiment
Aufklärungs-Abteilung
Panzer-Abwehr-Abteilung
Pionier-Bataillon
Nachrichten-Abteilung

Known war crimes

22 May 1940. Soldiers from *I.Regiment* killed 92 civilians in Aubigny-en-Artois.

22 May 1940. Soldiers from *II.Regiment* killed 45 civilians in Vandelicourt/ Berles-Montchel.

24 May 1940. Soldiers from *I.Regiment* and men from the *Totenkopf Pionierbataillon* killed 48 civilians in Beuvry.

27 May 1940. Soldiers from *4.Maschinengewehrkompanie 14.Kompanie, 1.Battalion, II.Regimient* killed 97 British POWs at Le Paradis.

Soldiers from Totenkopf were involved in the killings of black French colonial POWs at Lyon in 1940.